A CALL TO Ministry

RECEIVING THE STAMP OF THE CROSS

*Paul's second letter
to the Corinthians*

IVAN T. BLAZEN

Pacific Press® Publishing Association
Nampa, Idaho
Oshawa, Ontario, Canada

Edited by Kenneth R. Wade
Cover art by Lars Justinen
Designed by Michelle Petz

Copyright ©1998 by
Pacific Press® Publishing Association
Printed in the United States of America
All Rights Reserved

Blazen, Ivan R., 1934-
    A call to ministry : Paul's Second Letter to the
Corinthians / Ivan T. Blazen.
        p.   cm.
    ISBN 0-8163-1581-7 (alk. paper)
    1. Bible. N.T. Corinthians, 2nd—Criticism,
interpretation, etc. I. Title.
BS2675.2.B595   1998
227'.306—dc21   97-45640
                                                CIP

98 99 00 01 02 • 5 4 3 2 1

Contents

Dedication

To beloved Deanna,
through joy and suffering.

Introduction

Second Corinthians is the most personal and intense of Paul's letters. The success of his mission to Corinth is on the line, and Paul pulls out all the stops in trying to bring the rebellious Corinthians under his wing again and to effect lasting reconciliation between himself and them. You can tell a struggle is going on between Paul and his converts and also within Paul himself as his emotions rise and subside, and he labors to speak not only his mind but his heart. He loves these people, but they are so difficult to deal with. His apostolic authority is under attack by them and by outsiders who influence them. What do you do with unruly children whom you love? Tenderness and sternness, defense and offense, humility and pride are all bound to be present in your reaction and approach.

Paul's external and internal struggle comes out in the nature of the Greek he writes. First Corinthians is relatively easy to read in Greek, but 2 Corinthians is tough. The style is rough and broken, just what we would expect from a highly sensitive man under intense emotion.

This deep agitation and concern for his converts is one of the reasons why 2 Corinthians is the least structured of Paul's writings. Two other reasons are involved as well. The first is Paul's own nature, which is called into play in the strongest possible way because of the conflict in this situation. Paul was a man of rapidly shifting moods, divergent modes of expression, and fluctuating experiences. One minute things could be going well, and the next they were faltering. How else could it be as Christianity, a totally different orientation to life, made inroads among the old religions, beliefs, and customs of the Roman world?

Paul was the center of the confrontation between Christianity and paganism. In himself he mirrored the conflict, one moment breathing a feeling of success or a sigh of relief, and the next a sense of hostility and rejection. Furthermore, Paul saw things only in black or white, that is, super black or super white! He was a man who, by nature and experience, was given to excess in expression.

Second, though all Paul's writings fall into the category of letters, 2 Corinthians is a letter in the fullest sense. In situations of conflict, emotion, and urgency, letters are often dashed off without necessarily having an outline in mind. The writer says whatever comes to mind without organizing thoughts, seeking for balance in sentences, or weighing all his words. Things are referred to that the original readers will readily identify and understand. Modern readers, however, have to exercise great historical imagination to comprehend the situation.

This is the way it is with 2 Corinthians. In this letter we have to look over Paul's shoulder and try to figure out just what was happening. It is not a carefully organized presentation of thought as in Romans or an orderly dealing with topics as in 1 Corinthians. Rather, it is a revelation of Paul's own spirit. In 1 Corinthians we are given insight into the heart of earliest gentile Christianity and an intimate look at a church Paul founded. In 2 Corinthians we have an intimate portrait of Paul himself and insight into his great, affectionate, but often broken, heart.

If there ever was a time when patience was needed in reading a biblical writing, it is with 2 Corinthians. The letter is quite repetitive. Paul mentions charges against himself in one place and then comes up with similar or further charges in another. Accusations against him constitute one of the threads running through the letter. Another thread is the frequent mention of his sufferings, and still another is self-commendation and "boasting." The reader must not tire of these, for by patiently observing the repetitions, one gets a sense of just how pervasive the issues between Paul and his converts and opponents were. We need to hang in there with Paul through all of his repetitions so we can feel the weight that was pressing upon him and his desperate desire to overcome all obstacles.

The greatness of 2 Corinthians lies in its view of the Cross. The Cross is that world-reconciling event (2 Cor. 5:19) that is able to create reconciliation between God and mankind and between people estranged from each other. It is also the event that characterizes the ministry of Paul. It is stamped upon his life and work, and he wants it to be stamped upon the lives of his converts. The present is the time of cross bearing, not the time of glory and power, as the Corinthians thought.

In all who are followers of the Crucified One, the Cross takes shape and becomes a witness through the sufferings and self-sacrifice they undergo in the service of Jesus.

As far as Paul was concerned, he had no other claim to fame than that he represented and bore the cross in his life and ministry. He knew that of himself, as he encountered difficult situations, he had only weakness. But when he was weak, then he was strong, for the resurrection power of God sustained him and empowered his ministry at just such times.

This book then, is about the stamp of the Cross on Paul's life and ours. When one bears this stamp, the imprint of the resurrection will be felt as well. When we as God's servants feel weak, He keeps us going through trials, engenders and vitalizes our testimony to Christ, and will at last bring us, His often suffering people, into His eternal presence.

The New Revised Standard Version will be used in all quotations from the Bible unless otherwise indicated.

Readers are strongly urged to begin their reading with the words of Scripture itself. The Bible passages mentioned with the title of each chapter should be prayerfully studied first. Then this commentary may serve to clarify what Paul was endeavoring to say.

Blessings on all of you who read and seek to discern what the Spirit says to the churches of today. May the Cross stamp our lives as we follow our crucified and risen Saviour. "If any want to become my followers, let them deny themselves and take up their cross daily and follow me. For those who want to save their life will lose it, and those who lose their life for my sake will save it" (Luke 9:23, 24).

*We do not need to move toward God to make
Him agreeable to us. He moves toward us to make
the pathway of our pain easier.*

Chapter 1

2 Corinthians 1:1-7

SUFFERING APOSTLE AND COMFORTING GOD

Events leading up to 2 Corinthians

Sometimes no matter how much you love, how good your intentions are, how deeply you hope and pray for better things, how fully you try to solve problems and answer questions, your best efforts do not succeed. That is the way it was with Paul in his relations with the Corinthians. He fervently hoped the writing of 1 Corinthians would heal the divisiveness in the new church, solve their serious ethical and theological problems, reestablish his authority as their spiritual father, and bring about reconciliation between himself and them. However, Paul's hope was not fulfilled immediately. Only after a stressful period and a painful letter and visit did the beginnings of reconciliation occur, as 2 Corinthians 1–7 shows. Then, just when things were improving, some self-styled apostles upset the apple cart by challenging Paul's apostleship and authority and seeking to draw the Corinthians away from him (chapters 10–13). The great controversy is very real, and Paul experienced it markedly in his ministry. However, he did not capitulate to the negative forces arrayed against him, and neither should we. Tears, pain, patience, hard work, and time are the necessary preconditions for reconciliation.

It is no accident that the initial characteristic of love discussed in 1 Corinthians 13 is long-suffering (13:4), and the final attributes described are bearing, believing, hoping, and

9

enduring all things (13:7). Indeed, when everything else seems to totter, love never fails (13:8) but continues on together with faith and hope (13:13). Thus love outlasts the powers arrayed against it and gains the ultimate victory. The indomitable spirit of Paul breathes through these words and urges us to "keep on keeping on."

The problems Paul had with the Corinthians are indicated by the way his letters and visits to them developed. After establishing the Corinthian church (Acts 18:1-18), Paul found it necessary to send a letter admonishing his converts to guard their new lives and relationships from the immorality of their pagan past (1 Cor. 5:9). This letter must not have been successful, for after receiving news from various sources about serious moral and theological problems in the church (1:11; 7:1; 16:17), Paul wrote 1 Corinthians. In this letter he stated that he was sending Timothy to them as his representative prior to his own coming again to deal with their arrogance (4:17-19). In chapter 16 he again mentions his plan to come to them after evangelistic work in Ephesus and tells them not to give Timothy a hard time when he arrives but to send him on his way in peace to report to Paul concerning the situation.

Clearly, Paul was worried about his converts. The problems obviously deepened and, notwithstanding great opposition to his evangelism in Ephesus (16:9), Paul interrupted his work there to make a painful, corrective visit to the church at Corinth (2 Cor. 2:1). Unfortunately, this second visit (12:14; 13:1, 2) did no good, for Paul found it necessary later to write an anguished, tearful letter (2:3, 4; 7:8), trying to turn things around. Would his distress over the Corinthians never end? He dispatched this letter with Titus (2:13; 7:13) and, unable to endure the stress of waiting for his return with news, set out to find Titus as he journeyed back (2:12, 13; 7:5, 13). Finally, good news! Titus filled Paul's heart with rejoicing over the church's concern for him and its repentant spirit (7:5-16). The church had even disciplined an offender (2:5-9; 7:11, 12).

With this burden lifted, Paul wrote 2 Corinthians with its

messages of apostolic defense and reconciliation (chapters 1–7), directions for one of the most important offerings in the history of the Christian church (chapters 8, 9), and a tough stand against the arrogant intruders who were attempting to despoil Paul of his apostolic authority, alter his message, and win over his converts (chapters 10–13).

Greetings (2 Cor. 1:1, 2)

As Paul opens his letter, he identifies himself as an "apostle of Christ Jesus." To be an apostle was to be one commissioned by Christ to deliver an authoritative message, a message backed up by resurrection power. This is a claim of great authority, and the Corinthians, prone to an independent spirit and critical of Paul as an apostle, needed to take his apostolic calling seriously. Paul was Christ's ambassador! He was appointed by Christ to preach Christ. However, it was not only to Christ that Paul looked as the source of his authority but to God the Father as well. It was "by the will of God" that he was Christ's emissary. To make such a statement challenged the Corinthians to fully acknowledge his calling, as well as those interlopers who claimed to be Christ's true emissaries and Paul an inferior servant at best (10:12; 11:5, 6, 21-23). Thus in 2 Corinthians 1:1 Paul takes the bull by the horns and begins a defense of his apostolic authority, which will occupy much of the letter. He does this not from an oversized ego but because he is under attack.

After naming Timothy as a cosender of the letter, thus setting him in authority as well, Paul says he is sending the letter to God's own people ("saints"), not only in Corinth but throughout the province of Achaia, of which Corinth was a part. What Paul says to the Corinthians is open to the scrutiny of all believers in the area. The Corinthians needed to be in step with others who had a like faith in Christ and the same spiritual father. They were to be responsible not only to themselves but also to the larger body of believers who would give witness to how Paul, the apostle of them all, was treated. Thus, a note of accountability is struck.

In Western Christianity today, where individualism and individual churches are so emphasized, this is of great relevance. We are all part of a larger whole, the body of Christ. It is to this whole group that Paul offers the grace and peace that are found in God the Father and the Lord Jesus Christ. If we all have received these gifts, then we all are one in Christ.

Praise to the God of comfort

Instead of his usual practice of praising the recipients of his letters for elements of their Christian experience (see 1 Cor. 1:4-7), Paul concentrates his attention upon God. He had gone through so much difficulty with the church after writing 1 Corinthians that even their renewed interest in him and the spirit of repentance they now manifested (2 Cor. 7:5-14) could not be his focus. That was reserved for God, who had been his mainstay when the rowing got tough. So Paul says "Blessed be God" (1:1), not "Blessed be you."

Because of the love shown to my dying father by certain Seventh-day Adventists in Croatia—their loving witness turned my father to the Lord and to the Adventist Church—I wanted to thank one of them. Politely, in the Serbo-Croatian language I said, "Thank you so much." The man I spoke to shook off my thanks and looking up, pointed toward heaven and said to our gracious God, "Thank You."

So Paul pointed away from humans to the source of all blessing and said, "Blessed be God." The word for "blessed" here indicates not only that God should receive our blessing but that He is worthy to be blessed. We could translate it "Praiseworthy is God, the Father of the Lord Jesus Christ." Blessing is not only something we give but that God innately deserves, because His fundamental nature is praiseworthy.

What we have here then is a form of the doxology, "Praise God from whom all blessings flow." The particular blessing Paul has in mind is God's comfort and encouragement during times of trial and suffering. God is called "the Father of all mercies and the God of all consolation." What a beautiful statement about God! He is not an angry God we have to appease by our offerings and placate by our sufferings but One who is filled with mercy toward us and the desire to bring us comfort. We do not need to move toward God to make Him agreeable to us. He moves toward us to make the pathway of our pain easier.

God does not cause suffering or remove all suffering, but He is with us during our suffering to bring us a comfort and encouragement the world cannot give. "Peace I leave with you, my peace I give unto you. Not as the world giveth give I unto you. Let not your hearts be troubled, neither let them be afraid" (John 14:27, KJV). These words were spoken by Jesus on an evening when He forecast persecution of His disciples as well as the coming of the Comforter who would be with them. The idea of divine comfort recalls God's call to "Comfort, O comfort my people" (Isa. 40:1) and God's promise "As a mother comforts her child, so I will comfort you" (66:13).

The word *comfort* is a significant word in 2 Corinthians 1:3-7, occurring nine times. The comfort of which Paul speaks, and that he himself experienced, is more than sympathy. It is at once a sense of divine caring and a gift of divine strength to persevere through the most difficult times. God has a purpose in mind when He gives us such comfort. According to verse 4, God "consoles us in all our afflictions, so that we may be able to console those who are in any affliction with the consolation with which we ourselves are consoled by God." God is interested in us individually, and what we learn of His care during our suffering is meant to be passed on to others who suffer. Incredibly, we become God's agents of comfort! As I place my hand on one who suffers, it is ultimately Jesus' hand that is placed there. What a high privilege! There is no greater calling than to be a channel of His grace.

Verse 5 gives an incredible thought. The sufferings of Christ did not end at the Cross, but because we are one with Him, His sufferings reach into our experience of ministry for others. Our lives as Christian workers are stamped by the crucified Christ. This is similar to what Paul says of himself in Galatians 6:17, "I bear in my body the marks [wounds] of Christ." In Colossians 1:24 Paul makes the remarkable statement: "I am now rejoicing in my sufferings for your sake, and in my flesh I am completing what is lacking in Christ's afflictions for the sake of his body, that is, the church." Indeed, he says he wishes to experience the fellowship of Christ's suffering (Phil. 3:10). There is a solidarity between Christ and the Christian. The crucified Christ is alive in the community of His followers as they experience His call to take up the cross and follow Him (Mark 8:34). What happened to Him in a real way happens to them (see John 16:20), and what happens to them also happens to Him (see Matt. 25:25 and Acts 9:4).

According to 2 Corinthians 4:10, 11, the persecuted Christian worker, such as Paul, always carries in his body the death of Jesus and is always being given up to death for Jesus' sake. But as the sufferings of Christ overflow into Christian experience, so does the comfort that the crucified, now-risen Christ gives. This is a comfort that is to be shared with others who endure the same kind of suffering (verse 6). This reminds us of 2 Corinthians 4:11, 12, where Paul says that when our bodies bear the cross, the life of Jesus is revealed, there too, and it is a life not only for ourselves but for others as well.

Unbearable suffering and resurrection deliverance (2 Cor. 1:8-11)

The theme of suffering and comfort is deepened in 1:8-11. Here Paul refers to an affliction he experienced in Asia. It was important to him for the Corinthians to be aware of this terrifying experience (1:8). Their knowledge of it would be significant for at least three reasons. First, as missionary and pastor, Paul had identified with them in their need for Christ and salvation. Now he longed to have the sympathy of those he cared for so much. The people need the pastor, but the pastor also needs the people.

Second, by knowing how hard his lot had been, they would

be prepared to appreciate all the more the God who is able to rescue those under severe affliction (1:10, 11) and who, by rescuing Paul from his near-death experience, clearly validated his apostolic calling. This rescue proved that God needed him, and the Corinthians did too. Third, if Paul could get through this kind of experience by the power of God, he could get past the destructive work of his opponents.

What was the trial to which Paul refers? Possibly an illness. Using the plural form, which Paul frequently does when referring to himself, he says that he had received the sentence of death *in himself*. This is suggestive of a life-threatening illness. However, the reference could be to some persecution or imprisonment or to a trial in which everything seemed to be against him. We cannot be sure. Paul mentions no particular incident and gives no details as to circumstances or specific location.

However, he does describe the inner nature and meaning of the experience. It was so unbearably crushing, he says, that he "despaired of life itself" (1:8) Indeed, it felt as if a death sentence had been passed upon him (1:9). The Greek words he uses are very descriptive. In verse 8 he literally says, "We were burdened according to that which goes beyond, beyond [our] power." The main verb of this sentence means "oppressed" or "weighed down." Like a ship sinking, he felt that he was plummeting into the depths. Just how heavy was the burden of this trial or affliction? Paul is fond of words that indicate superabundance, and here, in an expression identical to that used in Galatians 1:13 for the excessive nature of his persecution of the church, he says that the weight was beyond all measure, something that surpassed all description, that it was "beyond [his] power" to endure. He felt there was no way out of death itself.

The Greek word Paul uses for this utterly hopeless condition is related to the English word *aporia*, which refers to a state of bewilderment and perplexity or not seeing the way through (the literal meaning of the Greek word). However, the Greek term is a strengthened form of this word, making the English translation "despaired" a good equivalent. It was as if a death sentence had been rendered and Paul was waiting for his execution. The sword was about to fall.

I once went through an experience that felt something like this. A devastating situation was having its effects on my body. The stress was so great I was becoming ill. I went to the doctor, and after he talked with me and examined me, I was shocked to hear him say, "You are dying. If you keep on like this, you will be dead!" Sometimes life can be so unbearably hard that we do feel like a verdict of death hangs over our heads. At such times there is only one source of ultimate appeal—the life-giving power of God. That is exactly what happened to Paul. He tells us God allowed him to have this experience to teach him to place his reliance and trust not in himself but in God, who raises the dead (2 Cor. 1:9).

God is not the cause of our terrifying times, but He does use these occasions to lead us to depend on His saving power. In the midst of utter discouragement He can bring comfort; in the thick of deadly circumstances He can raise us to life.

Paul's logic in verse 9 is the same as in 4:7-12. Here he compares those who minister the treasure of the gospel to brittle clay jars. This makes it clear that the power that delivers from the most severe trials belongs to God and not to us.

In 1:10 Paul affirms that the God who rescued him from his deadly peril (literally "so great a death") will continue to do so in the ever new extremities that face him. The key to hope for the future for every Christian is remembering what God has done for us in the past. So Paul says, "We have set our hope that he will rescue us again." But incredibly, the rescue that will be *effected* by God's power alone will be *affected* by the prayers of caring human beings! As we can be agents of God's comfort to others (1:4), so we can be involved, by way of prayer, in God's deliverance of people in peril. Sometimes we wonder whether intercessory prayer works and why, but according to this verse, whether we understand it or not, we are called to engage in it.

It is clear that Paul believes that the prayers of God's

people will be answered. He says the result will be "that many will give thanks on our behalf for the blessing granted us through the prayers of many" (1:11). When God's people pray according to His will, a chorus of praise will be heard for what He has done.

Thus, while the themes of affliction and despair begin the introductory section of 2 Corinthians 1, praise for prayer's results closes it. This teaches us that the last word is never the adversity we face but our deliverance by God's grace. Praise be to God for His love and care, in answer to our earnest prayer!

Maybe we need to be up front with God, too, for He has made every attempt to clearly reveal Himself to us.

Chapter 2

2 Corinthians 1:12–2:4

BAD RAP, GOOD APOSTLE

Griping and grumbling

Christian life and service takes many twists and turns. A zigzag line represents it better than a straight one. Under the Lord's direction, plans may have to change and strategies be reinvented. If we could see the end from the beginning, we would see how the Lord has led us. As Ellen White has said:

> God never leads His children otherwise than they would choose to be led, if they could see the end from the beginning, and discern the glory of the purpose which they are fulfilling as co-workers with Him (*The Desire of Ages*, 224, 225).

We should not be stuck in our own plans but open to the Lord's leading. Paul was this type of person. He moved as the Spirit prompted.

Sometimes this mode of operation can get one into trouble with people. Criticism arises when expectations are not met. People sometimes gripe instead of patiently seeking to understand. Grumbling and complaining can become the order of the day.

Though we must always be genuinely humble before God and people, there are times when we must stand up for the integrity of our motives and actions. We may not be able to

18

answer every charge, but charges that could ruin one's ministry and the success of the gospel must be answered.

The core of the great controversy theme, so prominent in Adventism, contains charges made against the integrity of God. Through God's redemptive activities in history, especially in Jesus Christ, every charge will be answered. According to Romans 3:4, God will prevail when He is judged and will be proven true over against the falsehood of man.

But if the Master has been judged, how much more certainly will his servants be judged as well. What were the judgments the Corinthians raised against Paul?

First complaint: Paul is insincere (2 Cor. 1:12-14)

We can deduce the complaints made against Paul by looking at his answers. It is evident from 1:12-14 that the Corinthians had questioned his integrity. The matter is serious, for Paul begins his answer by referring to what he is proud of, which arises from the testimony of his conscience (1:12). It is as if Paul is in a court of law and has been called upon to give testimony about himself. When he mentions his conscience, it is almost as if he says: "I swear to tell the truth, the whole truth, and nothing but the truth." His conscience was clear. It seems he was always having to defend himself to his converts. That is why in 1 Corinthians he says that he counts it inconsequential to be judged by the Corinthians or any human court. He affirms that he does not even judge himself, nor is he aware of anything against himself (1 Cor. 4:3, 4).

So strong is Paul's consciousness of the purity of his course that he says he can boast about it (2 Cor. 1:12). Paul's boasting, which is an unusual and strong feature of 2 Corinthians (1:12, 14; 5:12; 7:4; 10:8, 13, 15-17; 11.10, 12, 16-18, 30; 12:1, 5, 6, 9) has caused some to think Paul was an arrogant person. The way he speaks about self-commendation seems to support this (3:1; 4:2; 5:12; 6:4; 10:12, 18; 12:11). However, when we look closely at Paul, we realize that his boasting is of a different order. He engages in something the Corinthians were very fond of—to teach them what true boasting or self-commendation should entail. Already in 1 Corinthians he had said that whoever boasts should boast in the Lord (1:31), and that one who really loves others does not boast (13:4). Furthermore, he chided those who did boast (4:6; 5:2). Now, in 2 Corinthians, he reiterates that boasting should be in the Lord (2 Cor. 10:17) and that those who commend themselves are not the ones approved, only those the Lord commends (10:18). That is why he says: "We do not dare to classify or compare ourselves with some of those who commend themselves. But when they measure themselves by one another . . . they do not show good sense" (10:12). Indeed some of Paul's self-emphasis amounts to this: "We are not commending ourselves to you again, but giving you an opportunity to boast about us, *so that you may be able to answer those who boast in outward appearance and not in the heart"* (5:12, emphasis supplied).

When Paul boasts, he does so in part to inform the Corinthian boasters, against whom he is reacting, that boasting is a foolish thing (11:16-18). To mimic someone can show how they appear to others.

When it really comes down to it, however, Paul's boasting reflects humility, not arrogance. He boasts not so much in his achievements as in his weakness (11:30) in order that the emphasis may be placed where it belongs—upon the power of Christ that is with him in his weakness and hardship (12:9, 10; 6:4-7). Paul's list of accomplishments amounts to a catalogue of his sufferings for the cause of Christ (11:23-29; 6:8-12).

In 2 Corinthians 1:12 Paul uses the Corinthian vocabulary of boasting to stress that he has acted with real integrity. His argument moves from the lesser to the greater. He says that his conduct has been above reproach toward the world and especially toward them. If he has acted honestly toward the world, they can certainly be assured he will do the same toward them, his very own spiritual children. Implied in what Paul says about being above board with them is his desire that they do likewise with him. Reciprocity is necessary for a genuine relationship to exist.

Two words characterize his conduct: (1) "frankness" (some manuscripts read "holiness," the state of separation from the ordinary) and (2) "sincerity." The Corinthians undoubtedly were questioning whether they could count on Paul in both word and deed. Is he the real McCoy, the genuine article?

Believing in an inspired Bible written partly by God's servant Paul, we today could never envision bringing charges against him and impugning his integrity and motives. This was not the case in the earliest days of the church though. Paul had to fight for every inch of his apostolic role. He was an embattled servant of God.

When he says in 2 Corinthians 1:12 that he acted first of all with frankness, Paul means that he was completely open with them, relating to them with utter candor. He didn't do or say anything he didn't mean. As his second word explicitly states, he was totally sincere. Where did this sincerity originate? Was it an innate quality of Paul as a human being? No, for Paul says that it is "of God" (hence we may translate the phrase "godly sincerity"). This is why Paul says that his mode of operation is "not by earthly wisdom but by the grace of God." This reminds us of 2 Corinthians 10:3, 4, where Paul says that he does not wage war according to human standards, for his weapons are not merely human but have divine power. For Paul, God's grace was not merely God's forgiveness but the power for Christian life and ministry. In 12:9 he actually equates God's grace with His power.

We can identify with Paul's courageous attempt to clarify the kind of person he was, but it is sad that he had to defend himself from false charges that went right to the heart of his being. It must have drained his spirit. To be a true Christian and servant of Christ is to stand for the right though the heavens fall—and sometimes they do.

When Paul says in 2 Corinthians 1:13 that he writes only what can be understood clearly when read aloud in the congregation, it is obvious that the Corinthians had claimed either that there was obscurity in Paul's way of communicating (see 2 Pet. 3:16) or, more particularly, that he was not clear about his intentions toward them, saying one thing but meaning another. This would fit in with the charge against him in 2 Corinthians 1:17 that he in the same breath could say both "Yes, yes" and "No, no."

However, Paul assures them that his intention was to be clear. In fact, he wants nothing less than that they "understand fully" (RSV), that is, "to the nth degree" (my paraphrase), as the latter part of verse 13 says. Some render this part of the verse "understand until the end," (NRSV), but this is not the best translation, for Paul is contrasting full understanding, which is his aim, with the partial understanding they have now (verse 14). The Corinthians had some grasp of what Paul was saying, but he had to admit that while he wrote with the intention of being understood, it is obvious their understanding was incomplete.

An illustration of how Paul was misunderstood is found in 1 Corinthians 5:9-12. In a letter no longer extant, Paul had told them not to associate with immoral people. They thought this was completely unrealistic—perhaps deeming Paul to be a bit wacky on this point—since it would mean they had to cut off all dealings with society. Paul clarified his meaning by stating that he was not referring to people outside the church—one would have to leave the world to accomplish this!—but to immoral people inside the church.

To understand and be understood is a glorious experience, but life is filled with many partial understandings and misunderstandings. Every Christian has the task of trying to understand the real meaning of others, and as far as possible, communicating with openness, clarity, and simplicity. Friendships, marriages, and family relations could be saved if we did this. Tensions between leaders and laity, administrators, and theologians could also be greatly eased and even wiped away. Maybe we need to be up front with God, too, for He has made every attempt to clearly reveal Himself to us.

In 1:14 Paul strikes a note of signal importance. He refers to the day of the Lord Jesus, which is the day of judgment and Christ's return. Paul's clear conscience in verse 12 must be interpreted in terms of the final judgment. As he faces this judgment, he says his conduct and motivations have been honest. This is the strongest appeal Paul could make to get his converts to stop criticizing him. Paul's appeal to the final judgment contains an inference for the Corinthians. Was their conduct toward him the kind that could pass muster in the scrutiny of the final assize? As he says a bit later in the letter, "All of us must appear before the judgment seat of Christ" (2 Cor. 5:10). Undoubtedly, Paul wished for the Corinthians what he prayed for the Philippians—that they would be found pure and blameless in the day of Christ (Phil. 1:10).

What Paul wishes with all his heart is that when the day of judgment comes, the Corinthians, instead of complaining against him, will find cause to take pride (boast) in him, just as he wishes to do of them (if they will just get off his back and replace censure with respect and appreciation). Paul's desire to boast about his converts is expressed beautifully in 1 Thessalonians 2:19, 20 when he says: "For what is our hope or joy or crown of boasting before our Lord Jesus at his coming? Is it not you? Yes, you are our glory and joy!" Paul believed that if he could not rejoice in his converts on that day, his work as an apostle would have failed. It has been said that "no man is an island, no man stands alone." Minister and congregation are one. There is a sacred interdependence.

Second complaint: Paul is a vacillator (2 Cor. 1:15-22)

What Paul has said in verses 12-14 is the introduction to the question of his cancellation of a promised visit to the Corinthian church. The general charge against him (he is not sincere) now becomes specific (he did not come to us when he said he would).

The details of Paul's itinerary are a bit difficult to ascertain with precision, but it looks as though Paul changed his mind a couple of times. According to 1 Corinthians 16:3-9, he intended to stay in Ephesus until Pentecost and then, after passing through Macedonia, to spend the winter in Corinth. However, deteriorating relations with the

Corinthians led him to change this plan and make a short, painful visit to Corinth from Ephesus implied by the fact that Paul did not later wish to make *another* painful visit (2 Cor. 2:1). After this he went to Macedonia and, instead of returning to Corinth from there, as originally planned, went back to Ephesus. It looked to the Corinthians as if he would not be coming back at all, leaving them high and dry.

They were very unhappy about this change and charged him with being a fickle-minded vacillator who took his cues from worldly policy and self-interest (1:17). They probably wondered whether he really cared for them and whether the gospel promises he had given them were as unreliable as he seemed to be. If you can't believe the messenger, how can you believe the message?

Imagine Paul having to respond to such grave charges! Here is how he did it. First, he denied the charges, declaring that he did not say "Yes and No" at the same time (1:18). He did not speak out of both sides of his mouth. His assurances were not worthless. Next, he argued that his mode of operation was backed up by the faithfulness of God (1:18). He and God were so united that he could be counted upon to be as faithful as God. Further, he appealed to Jesus, the Son of God, whom he proclaimed, as the guarantor of God's promises (1:19, 20). When you look at Jesus, you have the Yes of God, the faithfulness of God, embodied in a person. If God was not saying Yes to the human race, why would He have sent Jesus? In Him every promise of God is rendered certain. And that is why, instead of questioning God's promises, we say Amen, meaning "so be it" or "it is true," to God through Jesus Christ. God's Yes to us is answered by our Amen to Him.

By way of illustration, God had made great promises to Abraham (Gen. 15:1-5). His response was that "he believed the Lord" (15:6). The Hebrew word for "believed" is *aman*, from which we get the English word *Amen*. In Isaiah 65:16 God is called the God of Amen, meaning the God of truth. We can rely on Him and His messengers.

Finally, Paul sought to dissuade his distracters by referring to the Spirit who had been put into their hearts by God (2 Cor. 1:21, 22) and had established the legitimacy of Paul as an apostle and of his congregation. Not only the faithfulness of God (1:18) and the Yes of Christ (1:19, 20) but also the presence of the Spirit in Paul and the Corinthians certifies that the relationship between himself and his converts is good. Their unity in Christ should not falter now because of misapprehensions about Paul. It would continue under the guarantee of the Spirit.

The Holy Spirit functions in two ways here. First, it is a seal (see also Eph. 1:13; 4:30). Seals were used in ancient times to show to whom objects belonged. They were a sign of ownership and protection. Both Paul and the Corinthians belonged to one and the same caring God. Secondly, the Spirit served as a guarantee (also Eph. 1:14). The Greek word used here, *arrabon*, can mean both a guarantee or pledge, as well as a first installment. With the gift of the Spirit, Paul and his converts could be certain of a great inheritance to come (Eph. 4:30 speaks about being sealed for the day of redemption) and, at the same time, experience the down payment of those spiritual blessings that would flower into the fullness of God's kingdom at Jesus' coming (see 2 Cor. 5:5). The relationship between Paul and his converts was destined for eternity; in fact, eternity had already entered into time. The new creation was already making itself felt and making them new creatures in Christ (5:17).

What profound results this reality should have had for the Corinthians and Paul! Instead of suspecting his motives, they should have seen themselves as partners with him in God's eternity, with all its blessings. They would indeed be together again—forever! Furthermore, Paul had brought them the gospel message that, by their believing and saying Amen, had made all this possible. Why not trust and believe Paul now as he attempts to clarify the reason he had not come back?

Surely, if God brought Paul to them in the first place, it must be God who was behind Paul's change of plans. As Paul said in 1 Corinthians 16:7, "I hope to spend some time with you, *if the Lord permits*" (emphasis supplied). Paul's ministry and timetable were under God's direction. He had wanted to see the Thessalonians again, but in their case, Satan had blocked the way (1 Thess. 2:17, 18). He had wanted to go to Rome for years but the immediate needs in other places had hindered him (Rom. 1:10; 15:18-23). Certainly, there had to be a reason why he had not yet returned to Corinth.

Paul's explanation for changing plans (2 Cor. 1:18-23)

As Paul had appealed to the testimony of his conscience (1:12) and the faithful support of God (1:18), he here calls upon God to witness against him in judgment against his very life (the meaning of the Greek) if what he is about to say is not true (1:23). Defending himself against the Corinthians was tough work, and Paul was leaving no stone unturned.

Paul vows that it was pastoral concern for the Corinthians that led him to abandon his original plans. "It was to spare you that I did not come again to Corinth" (1:23). Spare them from what? From making another painful visit, as he did from Ephesus (13:2). Painful to whom? Chapter 2, verses 2 and 3 make it clear that he did not want to cause them pain or suffer pain himself from those who really should have been causing him to rejoice. It is clear from verse 2 that another visit would necessarily have involved a very painful confrontation. He later says: "I warned those who sinned previously and all the others, and I warn them now while absent, as I did when present on my second visit, that if I come again, I will not be lenient" (13:2).

To cause the Corinthians the unavoidable pain of such a visit would also have cut Paul to the quick. For all his toughness, Paul had a sensitive nature. His converts were his joy, and if they were to hurt, even necessarily, he would hurt as well. Any mother or father who loves their child knows how much it hurts to discipline them.

So, wanting to avoid pain and yet give needed correction, Paul tried another strategy. He wrote them a letter (2:3, 4). It was a tough letter (one that made them grieve but only briefly, 7:8) so that when he came again, the hard things would be behind them (2:3).

I have often recommended letters rather than personal confrontations to those in marital and other difficulties. Sometimes a letter will work when nothing else will. It avoids meetings where tempers may run hot, real listening may not take place, or one person's statements may be cut off by the impatient counter remarks of the other. A letter written in a Christian spirit gives the reader a chance to process the ideas, dissipate anger by not having to gain the upper hand, and let off steam privately. This can prepare the way for real dialogue later.

However, as tough as Paul's letter was for them, it was rough on him as well. He wrote it "out of much distress and anguish of heart and with many tears." Its purpose, however, was not to cause them pain but to let them know the depth of his love for them (2 Cor. 2:4). To spare the rod and spoil the child is not really to show love. Even "the Lord disciplines those whom he loves" (Heb. 12:6).

In writing a letter and dropping his visit Paul avers that he was not trying to lord it over their faith (2 Cor. 1:24). In other words, by taking unilateral action, he was not seeking to coerce them in his direction, but he was working for their joy. Since their faith was firm in any case, coercion would not be successful.

We can learn much about the characteristics of real pastoral leadership here.

1. It is not afraid to discipline when necessary but uses severity as little as possible.

2. At the same time, the one who must exercise discipline does not do so in detached objectivity but identifies with the people. Tears will be in his eyes and heart.

3. It does not try to lord it over the flock, but because people of faith are being dealt with, seeks to gain their willing understanding.

4. Its purpose is to bring joy on the other side of sorrow and, through discipline, to manifest love for the people.

5. It maintains an attitude of faith and confidence that

the outcome will be good. As Paul says, "I am confident about all of you" (2:3).

On the other side of the fence, the congregation should not prejudge the pastor but listen carefully, giving him or her opportunity to explain. Members should not attribute insincerity to their pastor unless the evidence is overwhelming. Congregations should attempt to lighten the burden of pastors and bring them joy (2:3). Sanctified reciprocation between pastors and people should be the order of the day in our churches.

Chapter 3

2 Corinthians 2:5-17

THE FORGIVENESS AND
FRAGRANCE OF CHRIST

Painfulness and permissiveness

Paul talked a lot about pain in 2 Corinthians 2:1-4. He didn't want the kind of pain a head-on collision would have caused for everyone if he visited them once more. He had already had one sorrowful visit and did not want another. Instead, he wrote them a painful letter that would make their discipline easier to handle.

What was this letter about? It is clear from verse 5 that someone in the Corinthian congregation had caused distress to Paul. Paul states that the issue was larger than that. To criticize him was to cause pain to all his converts as well. In verse 9 he adds that he wrote to test whether they would be obedient to him in everything. It must be, then, that Paul's painful letter challenged the Corinthians to take action against someone who had made life miserable for him. Apparently this person had opposed and insulted him in an attempt to discredit him. That Paul had to write them about this shows that, as in the case of the incestuous man of 1 Corinthians 5:1-5, the church tolerated the offender. It just sat by and did nothing. The permissive Corinthians had allowed the belittling conduct toward the church's founder to stand. Such tolerance of evil in its midst would undermine the credibility, witness, and life of the church. Unchecked, this could lead to a greater outbreak of dissension in the church that was already famous for this very problem.

29

The unnamed offender

Who was this offender needing discipline? Some have thought it was the immoral person of 1 Corinthians 5:1-5 who, having been excommunicated from the church by Paul's direction, launched a personal vendetta against Paul. This is not likely, for if this man was now on the outside of the church, how could he be pictured in 2 Corinthians 2 as being inside it and requiring discipline? He had already received his punishment by being removed from the congregation.

Undoubtedly, Paul has another person and incident in mind here, but we have no idea who it was, for Paul, as a good pastor who cared for his flock *and the offender as well*, does not mention his name. Remember, there were no computers, copy machines, or printing presses in those days, so Paul's letter would have to be read aloud to the church. Paul did not want to have the man's name repeated in public even though he had publicly hurt him. No tit for tat with Paul. The spirit of Christ ruled in his life.

Church discipline and its function

As 2:6 indicates, the permissive Corinthian congregation heeded Paul's injunction and took formal disciplinary action against this person. Not everyone agreed, but the majority view prevailed, and an appropriate punishment was administered. The Greek word used here for punishment could mean anything from the severest penalty, excommunication, to exclusion from offices or rites of the church, on down to rebuke, censure, or reprimand. The punishment of Paul's reviler was probably not the lighter of these alternatives, for in verses 6 and 7 Paul said that the punishment was enough and the man needed comfort lest he be overwhelmed by excessive sorrow. This means the punishment must not have been excommunication either, for then he would have already felt excessive sorrow. Consequently, the action of the church involved some kind of temporary exclusion from aspects of the church's life. In any church this may at times be necessary.

The Corinthians were given to extremes. In this case, as

in 1 Corinthians 5:1-5, they at first did nothing. Then, when urged by Paul to take necessary and appropriate measures, they acted. But Paul's words imply that they got on a punishment kick and, had he not intervened, their retributive actions would have overwhelmed the man (2 Cor. 2:7) and given Satan, who was just waiting with all sorts of designs, a chance to take him over (2:11).

Therefore Paul ordered: It is enough! Punishment should be remedial, not merely retributive. So what should they now do? As forcefully as Paul had charged them to discipline, he now enjoins them to forgive the man, console him, and reaffirm their love for him (2:7, 8). Paul's word for forgive here contains the word for grace in it (*charizomai* is the verbal form of *charis,* which means grace). They should extend to the man a gracious (not grudging) forgiveness, attempt to heal his wounds, and in every possible way give him evidence of their love. This is reminiscent of Galatians 6:1, 2, which instructs that if *any* person be caught in *any* trespass (no matter what kind of sinner or what kind of sin), spiritual persons (those possessing the fruit of the Spirit, including love, patience, kindness, and gentleness—Gal. 5:22, 23), should gently mend the broken life of such a person.

Thus restoration and healing is the goal of all church discipline. Paul had expressed that very point in 1 Corinthians 5:1-5. There he said that the ultimate purpose of releasing a person from the fellowship of the church was that this might lead to an awakening of conscience and repentance and thus to salvation in the day of the Lord Jesus (5:5).

Paul's command to stop punishment, forgive, console, and love the injurer shows the greatness of his Christian heart. The center of the gospel—the compassion of God in forgiving sinners through Jesus Christ—motivated Paul at the core. Instead of vengefully wishing to increase the tempo of punishment in the name of his own honor and wounded pride, he embodied Jesus' admonition, "Love your enemies, do good to those who hate you, bless those who curse you, pray for those who abuse you" (Luke 6:27, 28). He was being guided by his own counsel, "Do not be overcome by evil, but overcome evil with good" (Rom. 12:21).

If Paul were alive today, he undoubtedly would advise members of all church boards to follow this course in disciplinary cases. To focus on correction rather than vengeance, transformation rather than mere retribution, love rather than hate—this is the only way the church, without hypocrisy before the God whose compassion has encompassed it, can remain Christian and witness to the power of Christ's love in the world.

Paul doggedly maintains that his concern in the discipline and forgiveness of the one who injured him is not merely personal but corporate. He asserts that the primary hurt is not to himself but to the congregation. Perhaps the minority, who did not support any discipline, thought the matter was not worthy of a corporate judgment, being just a private spat between Paul and one of his detractors. Not so, according to Paul. To slander a church leader affects not only the leader but the church he leads (2 Cor. 2:5).

This corporate injury is behind Paul's words in verse 10: "Anyone whom you forgive, I also forgive." This presupposes that the church body, not merely its apostle, has been wounded. And then he says, as if to minimize any personal significance, "What I have forgiven, *if I have forgiven anything* . . ." (2:10, emphasis supplied). Further, his role in the forgiveness, as minor as it may be in comparison with their forgiveness, "has been for *your sake* in the presence of Christ" (emphasis supplied).

The object of Paul's call for the community to forgive the offender was to keep the church from being outwitted by Satan, who stands ready with a thousand ploys to take over every person he can (2:11). Thus forgiveness, consolation, and love for sinners keep Satan from having his way! That means that mere condemnation and rejection of those who have done wrong gives Satan supreme advantage over the sinner and entree into the church! Let the church beware when it contravenes the gospel in the interests of a nontransformational retaliation against wrongdoers. What would happen to all of us who are sinners if God treated us this way, with strict justice but no mercy? We surely wouldn't be around to judge anyone else!

Impatient apostle (2 Cor. 2:12-17)

The Corinthians thought that since Paul had not visited them as promised, he did not care for them. Little chance of that, for Paul was so anxious to find out how things were between him and them that he could not wait for word but dispatched Titus to find out. When he came to Troas, even though God had opened the way for him to preach the gospel there, he could find no rest in his spirit because of his concern for the Corinthians. Even when engaging in promising evangelism, his pastoral heart could not stop ticking for those already converted in Corinth. This is a good lesson for evangelists. Their work is not only to reach new converts but to shore up the old.

So when Titus did not appear in Troas with a report, new interests did not block old concerns, and Paul set out for Macedonia. Second Corinthians 7:5 continues the story. There we see Paul still without rest, for the afflictions he was experiencing, "disputes without and fears within," were making him disconsolate. But when he met Titus and heard his good report, he finally found comfort. Did Paul love the Corinthians? *Dear Corinthians, just take a look at the facts. Paul suffered with care for your well-being.*

Triumphant God (2 Cor. 2:14-16)

From the mood of deep human anxiety expressed in 2.13 Paul suddenly shifts to thanksgiving to God. He has been thinking about himself; now he focuses upon God (2:14).

In our moments of deepest gloom there is none other than God to turn to, and we must turn to Him in faith, for outwardly things may seem to be caving in. Faith is the answer to fear. Paul's focus upon God in the midst of his frailty illustrates what he says later in the letter: "Whenever I am weak, then I am strong" (12:10). Only a connection with God can bring strength and elicit praise in the midst of adversity.

What is Paul thankful for? Not that God always causes him and his associates to triumph (as in the KJV translation). Paul is anything but triumphant at this point, but he is thankful that God leads the misunderstood, often rejected, and suffering apostolic group in *His* victory procession. Paul is probably alluding here to Roman victory processions after success in battle (see *The Acts of the Apostles*, 326). The conquering general, with incense perfuming the way, entered Rome through the triumphal arch, paraded through the streets of the city with an entourage of both celebrants and captives. After sacrifice was offered to the god Jupiter, who had made possible the defeat of the enemy, the prisoners were executed. For those who celebrated, the incense and smoke of sacrifice were an aroma of victory, but to those taken captive, a smell of their coming death.

Paul seems to make use of this custom in describing his apostolic life. In doing so he mixes metaphors and gives us an unexpected picture. He and his partners in ministry are not the celebrants in the procession but the captives, and it is for this captivity that Paul gives thanks! This is parallel to the picture in 1 Corinthians 4:9. In contrast to the mighty and wise Corinthians, Paul says that "God has exhibited us apostles as last of all, as though sentenced to death, because we have become a spectacle to the world, to angels and to mortals."

Paul and his co-workers have been taken captive to Christ (Paul often calls himself a slave of Christ) and have suffered humiliation and ridicule, persecution and pain from those they were commissioned to help. They seem to be bound for death. Indeed they have felt the power of death at work in them (2 Cor. 1:8, 9; 4:10-12).

Notwithstanding this ill treatment, they are the fragrance that spreads the knowledge of God everywhere. God triumphs over the weakness and rejection of his servants and uses them to reveal Himself to the world. What greater calling than to be a fragrance that scents the world with the beauty of Christ the Saviour!

As in the Roman procession, this fragrance or aroma has

a twofold effect: to one group, the gospel message from the lips and lives of God's messengers is a fragrance that brings life and only life (the force of the Greek phrase); to another it results in nothing but death. Life or death. What makes the difference and divides the world into those being saved and those perishing (1 Cor. 1:18; 2 Cor. 4:3)? Not self-effort, personal worthiness, greatness or power; only faith which perceives in the crucified Christ, represented through His suffering messengers, the wisdom and power of God, not the foolishness of man (1 Cor. 1:24). It is to recognize that God "is the source of your life in Christ Jesus, who became for us wisdom from God, and righteousness and sanctification and redemption in order that, as it is written, 'Let him who boasts, boast in the Lord' " (1:30, 31).

Sufficiency for ministry (2 Cor. 2:17)

So staggered is Paul by the awesome issues of his ministry—people eternally saved or eternally lost—that he is moved to ask at the close of 2 Corinthians 2:16, "Who is sufficient for these things?" The expected answer is, "No one!" Paul felt neither sufficient nor worthy (1 Cor. 15:9). His emotion-laden question is sincere as he reflects on himself as a minister. However, his words may also have a polemical edge. He is hinting that he stands in contrast to those false apostles, mentioned in 2 Corinthians 10–13, who came into the church peddling their own message and trying to undo Paul's work by snatching his converts for themselves.

It is undoubtedly with respect to these persons, who had cast aspersions on the integrity of his ministry and message, that Paul writes 2:17. He makes a number of claims in this verse. First, he is not a peddler of God's Word, as obviously was charged against him. There were wandering wisdom teachers in those days who profited by ripping off the people. The charge arose that Paul was not a real apostle but a con artist and peddler of words who takes financial advantage of his listeners. Paul's answer is a firm denial and a countercharge that others are the real hucksters and profiteers.

Second, Paul stresses once again, as in 1:12, that sincerity or purity of motive characterizes his ministry. His sincerity is a product of being in a vital union with Christ, which puts Christ in the center of his ministry. While this says something about himself, it is also a swipe against his accusers, who are really the insincere ones. With their different Jesus (11:4), how could they hope to find a sincerity that comes only by intimate connection with Christ?

Lastly, as Paul has focused on Christ, he now focuses on the Father. He claims a commission directly from God and carried on in God's presence. He knows that God is his Judge, and this certainly means, as he said in 1 Corinthians, that he wants to be a trustworthy steward, for he knows the day is coming when God "will bring to light the things now hidden in darkness and will disclose the purposes of the heart" (4:1, 2, 5).

Paul has begun to answer his question about sufficiency in 2 Corinthians 3:17. The answer, to be developed further in chapter 3, is that only one commissioned by God, under the authority of God, in a relationship with Christ, and manifesting sincerity of heart could ever hope to be sufficient to work for the Lord.

Realizing the overwhelming magnitude of the work, Paul exclaimed, "Who is sufficient for these things?" Who is able to preach Christ in such a way that His enemies shall have no just cause to despise the messenger or the message that he bears? Paul desired to impress upon believers the solemn responsibility of the gospel ministry. *Faithfulness in preaching the word, united with a pure, consistent life, can alone make the efforts of ministers acceptable to God and profitable to souls* (*The Acts of the Apostles*, 326, 327, emphasis supplied).

*It should never need to be said, as Ghandi once did,
"I like your Christ, but I don't like your Christians.
They are so unlike your Christ."*

Chapter 4

2 Corinthians 3

MINISTERS OF A NEW COVENANT

Letters of recommendation

As a minister and university teacher, I have often been asked to write letters of recommendation—for entry into various educational programs and schools, for scholarships, jobs, and mission service. These letters have value, since the candidates are not really known by those to whom they apply. When I agree to recommend someone, I give them my best shot. Sometimes by what I write they may come to look larger than life, and it may be thought that I have built them up too much. It is possible to go overboard and idealize an individual. In any case, the letters are important, for they introduce the person.

Paul recommended Phoebe to the Roman church (Rom. 16:1, 2) and had letters of recommendation written for himself during his career. As a rabbi, when he was chasing Christianized Jews all the way from Jerusalem to Damascus, he needed recommendations from the chief priests allowing him to bring those he caught back to Jerusalem to face the music over their newfangled faith, which seemed a threat to Judaism and its way of life under law (Acts 9:2; 22:5). His work on behalf of the law was in actuality a ministry of death, for under his influence and with his approval, these persons were punished, incarcerated, and even put to death. This point is of importance as a background to his discussion of the relation of the law to death in 2 Corinthians 3.

37

Letters of recommendation, while generally having significance, may be the product of political moves and used to bolster false authority. That is Paul's concern in 2 Corinthians 3:1, 2. As this chapter opens, Paul asks his readers if it sounds like he is trying to commend himself by affirming that he is a person of sterling motives, whose commission is directly from God and whose work can withstand the scrutiny of God's presence and judgment (2:17). He hopes the Corinthians will not understand him as promoting himself for, as he says in 3:1, "Surely we do not need, as some do, letters of recommendation to you or from you, do we?"

The little phrase "as some do," opens a large window on what was going on in Corinth. Because of the larger context of 2 Corinthians, especially chapters 10–13, it is clear that there were persons who had entered the church of Corinth with a spirit of self-commendation (10:12) and letters of recommendation to bolster their authority as true apostles over against Paul, whom they saw as unapproved. Paul sarcastically calls them "super-apostles" (11:5) and rebukes them saying they are false, deceitful persons, who pretend to be apostles of Christ (11:13). While identifying themselves as Christians and servants of Christ (11:23), they laid claim to a strong Jewish pedigree, calling themselves descendants of Abraham (11:22). Their understanding of Jesus and the gospel differed from Paul's, and the Corinthians seemed to be buying their views (11:4). Paul fears his converts will be led astray from a sincere and pure devotion to Christ (11:3).

So, as we read 2 Corinthians 3, we need to remember that Paul has his eye on his opponents and writes the way he does because he has their adversarial message and mission in mind. This chapter is written within the context of conflict.

I have sometimes wondered what Paul would have written if he didn't have any threats to his ministry and no one to argue with! But then again, to have what Paul wrote when his heart was breaking with pain, his spirit agitated over his converts, and his mind striving to defend his message is perhaps a better way to see the essence and importance of the gospel. In situations of conflict the gospel has to be most clearly articulated—what it is and is not forthrightly stated.

Over against his adversaries who could appeal to actual letters of recommendation (it would be interesting to know who wrote them!), Paul says he doesn't need such letters. Then, unexpectedly, he asserts that he has a letter he doesn't need! It is an unusual letter, for it is not external, like those of his opponents, but internal; not written with ink, but with the Spirit of the living God; not on stone tablets but on fleshly hearts (3:3). What is this letter, who wrote it, how was it delivered, and on whose hearts was it written?

Paul says to the Corinthians, "You yourselves are our letter" (3:2). The existence of a congregation of believers was a monument to God's hard working servant. People came into a saving relationship with Christ and became a part of the body of Christ, filled with the gifts of the Spirit, through the proclamation and ministry of Paul. The Corinthian church gave visible evidence of the legitimacy of Paul's ministry. Those we work for are our certification.

In verse 3 Paul goes deeper. Conscious of who the real creator of the church's life was, Paul specifies further: "You show that you are a letter from Christ, ministered by us" (my translation). Ultimately, the church is a reflection of the creativity and character of Christ. That it lives at all is due to Him, and if it lives in dependence upon Him and by the example of love He inspires, it is a recommendation for Him. Christ can only be seen in His followers; and a loving and lovable Christian is His greatest recommendation. It should never need to be said, as Ghandi once did, "I like your Christ, but I don't like your Christians. They are so unlike your Christ." Ghandi was able to look past the failing of Christians to see the goodness of Christ, but most people cannot.

In verse 3 the most intimate connection is made between Christ, the author of the letter, and Paul, who drew it up and delivered it. Let his critics know, in his ministry he has acted as Christ's secretary and letter carrier. The letter was entrusted to his care, not that of his opponents. Thus, as

Paul asserts the primacy of Christ, he establishes the place of his own ministry. If Paul's letter is actually Christ's, then he has a high place indeed.

Upon whose hearts is this letter written? It would seem at first glance that it would be the hearts of the Corinthians, and some Bible translations say "written on your hearts." There is some manuscript support for this. However, an even better translation is "written on our hearts." The Corinthians are the letter of recommendation written on Paul's heart.

A letter of recommendation is about the person bearing the letter—in this case Paul. It was his ministry that was being attacked and its legitimacy that was being affirmed by the very existence of the Corinthian believers. Wherever Paul goes, he carries their letter with him, that is, within his own heart. President George Bush said, "Read my lips," but Paul declared, "Read my heart." And he says in 7:3, "You are in our hearts." Out of his very heart, "to be known and read by all" (3:2), Paul can bring forth testimony of God's action through him. This is why he calls his converts his joy and crown (Phil. 4:1; 1 Thess. 2:19, 20). They were the crown he wore *on his head* and the letter that was *in his heart*.

Confidence and competence (2 Cor. 3:4-6)

Confident people are usually competent people. Confidence in oneself opens the door to competence, and competence inspires confidence. Paul was a confident person but not because he felt competent of himself. In verse 4 he says his confidence comes "through Christ"; it is not self-generated. Even further, the confidence Christ makes possible is exercised "toward God." Paul is confident in the God in whose presence he works (as in 2:17).

As Paul is confident in God, so his competence comes "from God" (3:5). So comprehensive was it that Paul refused "to claim *anything* as coming from us" (emphasis supplied). He was totally dependent upon God to empower him for service.

The word translated "competent" could also be rendered "sufficient." Paul's sufficiency was God-enabled. Interestingly, the Greek word behind "competent" or "sufficient" (*hikanos*), is used for God in the Greek translation of the Old Testament used by Paul in his missionary travels. El Shaddai, the "Sufficient One," in Hebrew becomes *ho hikanos* in Greek. Thus Paul's sufficiency comes from the "Sufficient One." He was qualified or made competent for his work from no less a source than "God Almighty." Though Paul speaks much about boasting in 2 Corinthians, he never boasted in what he had done but always in what God had done. He gave the glory to God. It was God's power that was made manifest in his weakness (12:9).

When our Christian experience seems to sag or we feel unable to accomplish what the Lord has given us to do or to go through the trials we have to face, let us remember that our sufficiency comes from God. We can ask of Him as did the elderly man who so meaningfully prayed: "Lord, prop me up in all my leanin' places." Our Almighty God surely will.

New covenant; old covenant (2 Cor. 3:6-11)

What had God qualified Paul for? To be a minister "of a new covenant, not of letter but of Spirit; for the letter kills, but the Spirit gives life" (3:6). It seems clear that with this contrast, Paul sets himself off from his opponents. They made a big point out of the fact that they were true-blue Jews (11:22) and must have called particular attention to Moses and the Mosaic economy. Otherwise, Paul would have had no special reason to contrast Moses and the administration of the law with the ministry of the Spirit in 3:6-16. Apparently they appealed to the law as of crucial importance for salvation. This harmonizes with the fact that they preached a different Jesus and gospel than Paul preached (11:4). Undoubtedly, as with the Corinthians generally, these Jewish Christians did not emphasize a Jesus who was crucified in weakness (13:4) but one whom they interpreted in terms of Moses, who saw the glory of God when the law was given. Jesus was probably looked upon as a kind of new Moses dispensing a new law rather than as a Saviour from sin.

I once had a seminary student who, as he thought of Paul's

statements on the law that at times seem negative, said to me: "I don't like Paul; I like Moses!" I think Paul's opponents in Corinth were something like that. Moses stands for upholding God's law and the obedience God asks. A central element of Moses' leadership was giving the law to the people. Influenced by the importance of God's law, Paul's critics found offense when Paul began to say things like: No one can be right with God through the law (Gal. 2:16; Rom. 3:20); Christ came to redeem those under the law (Gal. 4:5); we are no longer under the law (Rom. 6:14; Gal. 3:25); we have died to the law, and hence are dead to what held us captive (Rom. 7:4); the covenant of Sinai bears children for slavery (Gal. 4:24, 25); the law is a ministration of death, for the letter of the law kills (2 Cor. 3:6, 7); and we no longer serve God under the old written code (Rom. 7:6).

We as Seventh-day Adventists, raised up in part to show the centrality of the law in the great controversy and the continuing validity of the law in the Christian life, have sometimes had difficulty with such statements ourselves. We have appealed to a right idea, the distinction between moral and ceremonial law but may not have always used this correctly. This distinction, as valid as it is, does not explain all of Paul's statements. For example, to no longer be under law means something more than no longer being under ceremonial law. The letter that kills and the law as a ministration of death in 2 Corinthians 3 is not a reference to ceremonial law, for Paul speaks of the ministration of death as chiseled in letters on tables of stone (3:7), an obvious reference to the Ten Commandments. To no longer serve God under the old written code does not mean merely that we no longer keep ceremonial laws. The truth is deeper than that, for Romans 7:6 and 2 Corinthians 3:6, where this idea occurs, mention serving God in the Spirit. It is *how* we serve God that is the issue, and this is relevant for *all* law.

In 2 Corinthians 3:6-11 Paul is demonstrating the superiority of the new covenant to the old to show that those who are ministers of the new covenant (Paul and his associates) are superior to those who minister in terms of the old covenant (Paul's critics and rivals).

In what way, then, is the new covenant superior to the old? In answering this, we should acknowledge that not every New Testament passage dealing with the old/new covenant theme deals with it in the same way. (In addition to 2 Corinthians 3, see Gal. 3:15-25; 4:21-31; Heb. 7:22; 8:6-13; 9:1, 15, 18.) There are varying, but complementary, emphases based upon the specific problems being addressed. We must avoid the temptation to jam all the passages together in an endeavor to come out with a quick, general meaning. Each passage must first be allowed to make its distinctive contribution to the overall teaching of Scripture. So, what does 2 Corinthians 3, in its own context, say about the superiority of the new covenant to the old?

First, the old covenant, which is equated in this passage with the writings of Moses (3:14, 15) and the Decalogue (3:3, 7) is described in verse 3 as external (written on tablets of stone) in contrast to what is internal (written on human hearts). This means that the old covenant's distinguishing feature is "letter" (3:6, 7), whereas the central element of the new covenant is "Spirit" (3:6, 8). In the new covenant promise in Jeremiah 31:33, God promised to write His law (the code of Sinai) on His people's hearts, and in Ezekiel 36:26, 27 said: "A new heart I will give you, and a new spirit I will put within you; and I will remove from your body the heart of stone and give you a heart of flesh. I will put my spirit within you, and make you follow my statutes." Paul's way of saying this is: "We serve God not under the old written code [literally: not in oldness of letter] but in the newness the Spirit makes possible" (Rom. 7:6; my paraphrase). Ellen White's comments on this are moving:

All true obedience comes from the heart. It was heart work with Christ. And if we consent, He will so identify Himself with our thoughts and aims, so blend our hearts and minds into conformity to His will, that when obeying Him we shall be but carrying out our own impulses. The will, refined and sanctified, will find its highest delight in doing His service. When we know God as it is our privilege to know Him, our life will be a life of continual obedience (*The Desire of Ages*, 668).

The old covenant is a ministration of condemnation (2 Cor. 3:9) and death (3:6, 7), whereas the new covenant is one of justification (3:9) and life (3:6). How could the old covenant with its holy, just, and good law (Rom. 7:12) do otherwise than kill (2 Cor. 3:6; Rom. 7:9-11) or curse (Gal. 3:13) when its sacred provisions were broken by morally weak and sinful human beings? Ellen White has strongly stated:

If the transgressor is to be treated according to the letter of this covenant, then there is no hope for the fallen race; for all have sinned, and come short of the glory of God. The fallen race of Adam can behold nothing else in the letter of this covenant than the ministration of death; and death will be the reward of everyone who is seeking vainly to fashion a righteousness of his own that will fulfill the claims of the law. By his word God has bound himself to execute the penalty of the law on all transgressors (*Signs of the Times*, 5 Sept. 1892).

Over against this negative reality the new covenant brings God's pronouncement of acquittal and forgiveness for all our trespasses. In Romans 4, the great passage illustrating the nature of justification (or the reckoning of righteousness), Paul appeals in verses 6-8 to Psalm 38:1, 2 to define its meaning:

So also David speaks of the blessedness of those to whom God reckons righteousness apart from works: "Blessed are those whose iniquities are forgiven, and whose sins are covered; blessed is the one against whom the Lord will not reckon sin."

Then from the same chapter of Romans, Paul presents a

second aspect of justification. He speaks of God as He "who gives life to the dead and calls into existence the things which do not exist" (Rom. 4:17). The power of God at work both in creation (calling into being what does not exist) and resurrection (giving life to the dead) is at work in believers. We may feel dead in our trespasses and sins (Eph. 2:1), but the God of creation and resurrection speaks to us the word of life. Justification is always life-giving—as Paul tersely says in Romans 5:18. Indeed, "The Spirit of life in Christ Jesus has set you free from the law of sin and of death" (8:2).

In the third place the glory of the new covenant surpasses the glory of the old. Three times Paul uses the words "How much more" to indicate the greater glory of the new covenant when compared with the old (2 Cor. 3:8, 9, 11).

There was no question in Paul's mind that the old covenant was glorious. In fact it was so glorious that when Moses came down from meeting God and receiving His law, the people of Israel could not gaze at his face (3:7). Moses therefore veiled himself. The voil served not only the purpose of keeping the people from being blinded by the glory of the old covenant but also to keep them from "gazing at the end of the glory that was being set aside" (3:13). Paul teaches that paradoxically the glorious old covenant contained within it a hint of its own passing. It would be eclipsed by the greater and permanent glory of the new covenant (3:11). What Paul says here has the feel of John 1:16, 17. Comparing Jesus and Moses, John says: "The law indeed was given through Moses; grace and truth came through Jesus Christ."

What Paul has been saying about the nature and glory of the new covenant in contrast to the old has ramifications for the greatness of his ministry when compared with the ministry his opponents were carrying on in support of the old covenant. His ministry eclipsed theirs just as the gospel transcends and fulfills the law.

Boldness, freedom, and transformation (2 Cor. 3:12-18)
Still thinking of his opponents, Paul says that since he has the hope that comes from the new covenant (justifica-

tion, life, the Spirit, and God's law in his heart), he acts with great boldness—he gives his gospel message with authority no matter what his critics think—and does not need a veil over his face when meeting the people, as Moses did.

Now Paul makes an interesting switch. The veil that up to this point had been on Moses' face is now said to be over the hardened minds of the Jewish people and anyone like them who looks to the law for salvation or security. When these people read the old covenant (Moses' writings), there is a veil over them that is taken away only when they turn to the Lord and come to be "in Christ" (in a vital union with Christ). The law was glorious, but our focus must be solely on Christ and His glory. In fact, Christ is the true glory of the law. Only in Him does the law come to its fulfillment, and only in Him is it read aright.

I have a book written by a famous Jewish scholar who specializes in New Testament studies. Just as Jews through the centuries have done, he criticizes Paul for his doctrine of the law, for it departs from Jewish teaching. However, he admits that if he thought Jesus was the Christ, this would affect how he would understand the law. For Paul, Christ is the key to the meaning of the law. He is the One who, in His life and death, and in the life of every believer, fulfills what the law intended but by itself could not do (Rom. 8:3).

It is not just that Paul gives and defends the gospel boldly (that is, openly and honestly), instead of with a veil hiding his face, but to every Christian the Spirit of the Lord grants the freedom of boldness. This boldness allows us to approach God freely (see Heb. 4:16) and to give the message the same way—unafraid no matter what the opposition.

Paul's concentration in 2 Corinthians 3:18, however, is on the freedom of our approach to the Lord and what happens when we see His glory. Not only ministers but "all of us, with unveiled faces, seeing the glory of the Lord as though reflected in a mirror, are being transformed into the same image from one degree of glory to another." The unveiled faces of all, spoken of in this text, stand in contrast to the one person, Moses, who with unveiled face could see God, as well as to those who had a veil over their hardened hearts when reading what Moses wrote.

When the hardness is gone, the vision of the Lord becomes bright, and great effects follow. First, we see the glory of the Lord as though reflected in a mirror. The words *mirror* and *image* in this text are connected. In the light of 4:4, which speaks of "the glory of Christ, who is the image of God," we should understand Christ to be the mirror. We do not see God directly but only in the mirror of Christ, who perfectly reflects God. Second, by seeing the glory of God in Christ, we (unbelievably) are transformed into the same image. The only way the world can see the glory of God in Christ is for us to mirror Christ in our lives. Believers are the little mirrors of God!

In 2 Corinthians 3 Paul takes us all the way from condemnation and death by the law to justification, life, and transformation by the Spirit. The end of the line is being like Christ, whose image is formed in us through His Spirit (3:18). There are no spiritually elite in the New Testament. "All of us, with unveiled faces" may have this experience.

The law cannot transform a person, but the Spirit can when we have come into vital union with Christ. This transformation, in contrast to the fading glory of the old covenant, is an increasing reality in the life of those who are joined to Christ. We move "from one degree of glory to another." This means that every day brings new conformation to Christ (compare Rom. 8:29). However, it may also mean "from the advancing glory of this life to the final glory of being with Christ." Some may claim to have arrived—the Corinthians certainly made such a claim (1 Cor. 4:8)—but there is no stopping point in growth in Christ and likeness to Him. Finally He will come, and we shall be like Him (for we shall see Him as He is—1 John 3:2) and be forever with Him. To be like Christ and with Christ—this is the goal of the Christian life.

Can author and readers sing together? Let's imagine we can and sing the following stanzas of two moving hymns.

When We All Get to Heaven
Let us then be true and faithful,
Trusting, serving every day;
Just one glimpse of Him in glory
Will the toils of life repay.
When we all get to heaven,
What a day of rejoicing that will be!
When we all see Jesus,
We'll sing and shout the victory!

Onward to the prize before us!
Soon His beauty we'll behold;
Soon the pearly gates will open—
We shall tread the streets of gold.
When we all get to heaven,
What a day of rejoicing that will be!
When we all see Jesus,
We'll sing and shout the victory!
(*Seventh-day Adventist Hymnal*, 633)

The Glory Song
When all my labors and trials are o'er,
And I am safe on that beautiful shore,
Just to be near the dear Lord I adore,
Will through the ages be glory for me.
O that will be glory for me, glory for me, glory for me;
When by His grace I shall look on His face,
That will be glory, be glory for me.

When, by the gift of His infinite grace,
I am accorded in heaven a place,
Just to be there and to look on His face,
Will through the ages be glory for me.
O that will be glory for me, glory for me, glory for me;
When by His grace I shall look on His face,
That will be glory, be glory for me.
(*Seventh-day Adventist Hymnal*, 435)

Until Jesus comes and the present evil age is no more, believers live between the times. They feel the greater presence of the new age, forgiving their sins and giving them the power of a new life, but also the continued impingement of the old age.

Chapter 5

2 Corinthians 4:1–5:10

EARTHEN VESSELS AND RESURRECTION POWER

The Glory of God in Jesus the Lord (4:1-6)

In every age there have been preachers who, in the interest of personal prestige and enrichment, would do almost anything to gain a following and get gain from their following. We have seen the specter of televangelists who, under the cover of being ministers for Christ, have committed adultery or built financial empires upon fraudulent claims.

Who would ever cast Paul in such roles as these? As a matter of fact, some in his time did just that. Their claims against Paul surface again in chapter 4.

However, before Paul deals with complaints against himself, he makes a positive statement about his apostolic work and his personal feelings resulting from it. He says: "Therefore, since it is by God's mercy that we are engaged in this ministry" (4:1). Here is the presupposition that guided Paul's life as an apostle. God's mercy was behind his new covenant ministry. Mercy is the essence of the new covenant, and it was by God's mercy that he was called to be an apostle. First Timothy 1:12-16 is illuminating in this regard. Here Paul shows how he formerly was a persecutor, a man of violence who acted ignorantly in unbelief. But, he says, God gave him mercy, and His grace overflowed into his heart with the love that is in Christ Jesus. In persecuting Christians he was the foremost of sinners, but God granted him mercy that he might become an example to those who would believe in Him for eternal life. Marvelous passage! God's mercy to Paul was twofold: It forgave his wrong and propelled him into a ministry of making people right with God. Paul never forgot that it was by the grace of God that he became what he was (1 Cor. 15:10).

Consequently, in 2 Corinthians 4:1 he says that, as a result of God's mercy leading him into ministry, he does not lose heart. He does not grow weak or weary and just give up, though there were plenty of things over which he could have thrown in the towel.

I remember a wonderful colleague who, upon unjustly receiving a deflating attack of criticism, dropped out of sight for days. No one heard from him or could reach him. He was too discouraged for contact. He had devoted his life to the work of the church, and the criticism was totally contrary to his consciousness of his calling and quality of work over the years. We need to deal with people with utmost tact, concern, and willingness to hear them out before we make our judgments. We should also recall Jesus' statement, "Judge not that you be not judged" (Matt. 7:1, RSV).

In any case, no matter what the barrage of criticism, Paul knew what kind of ministry he had, how he got it, and its transforming power in his life, bringing him into ever great harmony with the image of his Lord (2 Cor. 3:18). He had gained a spirit of freedom and boldness as a result (3:17) and did not lose heart.

But regardless of God's leading in his life, Paul's critics were still there. In response to them he made three denials: He did not have any shameful deeds to hide; he did not cleverly deceive people; and he did not adulterate the word of God. On the contrary, these were the kinds of things his opponents were involved in.

As a young minister some years ago, a man came to me, trying to win my backing, saying that his wife had committed adultery against him. He brought advocates with him. In my inexperience, I bought his story hook, line, and sinker. Was I ever surprised to discover that *he* was the perpetrator of the adultery, not his wife. He came to me, among others, to get a sympathetic support group with which to browbeat his wife into silence and submission. The loudest critics are sometimes the greatest sinners!

Paul's rebuttal to the charge of deception and falsifying God's Word is that "by the open statement of the truth we commend ourselves to the conscience of everyone in the sight of God" (4:2). Truth is Paul's only commendation, and he speaks it in the full consciousness of God's presence and watchful eye. This reminds us of 2:17, where Paul says he speaks sincerely in the presence of God, who gave him his mission. If we could all maintain a sense of God's presence, it would change the quality of our words and actions.

The idea of the open statement of truth stands in opposition to the charge in 4:3 that Paul's gospel was veiled, that is, unclear, misleading, or without the light of truth. Paul had already argued in chapter 3 that in Christ the veil that obscures the meaning of God's word is removed. Consequently, the charges of his critics that his gospel was veiled must have been the result of two fateful factors: They were among the perishing, and the god of this world had blinded their eyes—they had the hardened, veiled minds spoken of in 3:14, 15—keeping them from seeing the light of God's glory in Jesus (4:4).

The idea of the god of this world blinding people sits strangely with the concept that in Christ there exists a new creation (5:17) and that today is the day of salvation (6.2). There is a great controversy going on here. The antagonists are Satan, the god of this world, and Christ, the author of the new creation and giver of salvation. If Satan is ruler of this age, how can there be a new creation and the presence of salvation? How can both of these realities exist at the same time?

To understand this we must recall that common to Judaism and early Christianity was the doctrine of the two ages. This included the present age or world (Gal. 1:4; 1 Cor. 1:20; 2:6, 8) and the age to come (Heb. 6.5; Eph. 2:7). Sometimes both ages are mentioned in the same text (Matt. 12:32; Luke 18:30; 20:34, 35; Eph. 1:21). The present age is dominated by evil and the working of Satan, and the age to come is the golden age when God's kingdom will hold complete sway. For Judaism the age to come follows this age, but for the New Testament the two overlap. One of the markers for the age to come is the resurrection, and this already has begun with the resurrection of Jesus, who is the first fruits of those who sleep (1 Cor. 15:20). Thus the new age is already present in the midst of the old (it will be fully present when Jesus comes again) and delivers people in the here and now from "the present evil age" (Gal. 1:4) through the death and resurrection of Jesus. Nevertheless, as with the parable of the wheat and tares growing together until the end (Matt. 13:36-43), the power of evil still makes its presence known, and the prince of darkness still works.

We may represent the relation of the two ages by two intersecting circles, one larger than the other to represent the greater power of Christ's kingdom over Satan's kingdom. Until Jesus comes and the present evil age is no more, believers live between the times (where the two circles overlap). They feel the greater presence of the new age (please note that this usage of the term "new age" has nothing to do

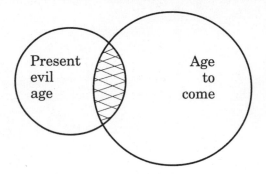

with the modern New Age movement, which is founded largely on spiritualism), forgiving their sins and giving them the power of a new life, but also the continued impingement of the old age. Temptation still abounds. Outside of Christ, one is exclusively in the old age of which Satan is the god.

This is how Satan's rule and the new creation can coexist. It is our choice which realm we want to belong to.

According to Paul, the god of this world has blinded the minds of unbelievers. Satan does not wish people to see "the light of the gospel of the glory of Christ, who is the image of God" (2 Cor. 4:4). His constant effort is to keep our eyes off Christ, for in Him we discover who God is and what He does for our salvation. When we look at Jesus, we see what God is like. Christ, as the image of God, makes visible the invisible God (Col. 1:15). According to Hebrews, Christ "is the reflection of God's glory and the exact imprint of God's very being" (1:3). And Jesus says, "Whoever has seen me has seen the Father" (John 14:9).

Paul declares that, in view of this truth, what he preaches is not himself but Jesus Christ as Lord (2 Cor. 4:5). Because Paul saw such a close connection between his gospel ministry and the Christ he proclaimed, his critics charged him with preaching himself. Paul denies this and says that he is only a servant, and Jesus Christ alone is Lord.

This statement about Jesus is at the heart of Christianity and may be taken as a confession of faith. The question it raises is, Who is Jesus? The answer is that He is Christ (our Saviour and Deliverer) and Lord (our Master and King). Here is the gospel in a nutshell. "Christ" is not the second half of Jesus' name but specifies His office and function. He has been anointed to bring deliverance to his people. In calling Him Christ (or Messiah), we emphasize what God does for us and His gift to us. To call Jesus Lord stresses what God asks of us, His claim upon us. Gift and claim are two halves of the total gospel message. By proclaiming only the first, one can be in danger of antinomianism (God's will doesn't matter). By proclaiming only the second, legalism may result (Christ's cross doesn't really make the difference; my lifestyle does). Seventh-day Adventists have been called to preach both, but in the right order. It is in the light of Christ's salvation that He calls us to obedience to Himself as Lord. We must not get the cart before the horse. Salvation is the horse and obedience the cart.

In 2 Corinthians 4:6 Paul describes how the God of creation, who said, "Let light shine out of darkness" (Gen. 1:3 with 1:4, 5) has shone in his heart "to give the light of the knowledge of the glory of God in the face of Jesus Christ." Paul asserts that his conversion and subsequent ministry were like the first day of Creation when God created light and separated it from darkness. There was an appearance of the glorious, risen Christ to Paul on the Damascus road, and Paul was blinded by the light, but there was also an inner illumination and transformation of Paul by the glory of God in Jesus' face. When he saw that face, he was changed (compare 2 Cor. 3:18). Ellen White speaks of Paul's conversion and call to ministry as an "hour of heavenly illumination" (*The Acts of the Apostles*, 115). With great impact she says: "Upon the soul of the stricken Jew, the image of the Saviour's countenance was imprinted forever" (ibid.).

Should it not be the same with us? On the wall of my college dorm room was a large glass-covered painting of the face of Jesus. One day as I gazed reverently at the painting, the light reflected off the glass in such a way that I saw the outline of my face in the face of Jesus. My face was there, but what really came through was the face of Jesus.

We need to pray: "Oh Lord, may the face of Jesus be seen in me, not in such a way that people think I focus on myself but only in such a way that His face is given all the prominence and *He* is seen as *Lord*. To Him be the glory and praise forever."

Treasure in clay pots; life in mortal flesh (2 Cor. 4:7-12)

Paul says that the treasure of the gospel—the light of the knowledge of God's glory in Jesus (4:4, 6)—is contained in clay pots. This likely is a reference to the cheap pottery lamps made in Corinth and used for walking at night. They were very thin so the light could shine out, but this meant they could be cracked easily. Unlike pots made of glass or metal, these could not be repaired if broken. Thus they were fragile, without great value, and expendable. This is how Paul describes himself—he is nothing but a clay jar, easily cracked.

(It is one thing to be a cracked pot, as Paul's many hardships suggest he was; it is another to be a "crackpot," as his critics charged him to be!)

But, he asserts, though he amounts to very little, the transcendent treasure of the gospel shines through his weakness. In fact, by using such a fragile vessel as Paul, God was making it clear that the extraordinary power of the gospel belongs to Himself and not to any human instrument (4:7).

In the dual reality of weakness and power that characterized his ministry, Paul sees a replica of the death and resurrection of Jesus. It was precisely in the difficult and deadly aspects of his ministry that Paul experienced the resurrection power of God. The following chart of his words shows how the stamp of Jesus' death and resurrection was upon him.

Death of Christ	Risen Life of Christ
4:8 We are afflicted in every way,	but not crushed;
perplexed,	but not driven to despair;
4:9 persecuted,	but not forsaken;
struck down,	but not destroyed;
4:10 always carrying in the body the death of Jesus,	so that the life of Jesus may also be manifested in our bodies.
4:11 We are always being given up to death for Jesus' sake,	so that the life of Jesus may be manifested in our mortal flesh.
4:12 So death is at work in us,	but life in you (RSV).

Paul was not only the theologian of the Cross and Resurrection, but the bearer of these events in his own experience. His opponents made much of their powers, but he made much only of God's power in human weakness. This is the theme of 2 Corinthians as a whole. Paradoxically, but like Jesus, the death Paul bore himself (4:11) created life for his converts (4:12). As he says in 4:15, "Everything is for your sake."

What Paul meant by treasure in earthen vessels comes out clearly in verses 10 and 11, when he speaks of Jesus' life made visible in our bodies (4:10); that is, within our mortal flesh (4:11). Just think of it: Resurrection life is experienced in our *mortal* bodies. It seems like a contradiction—but only if the God of creation is left out of the picture. With God all things are possible, and He can renew our lives in the very midst of our suffering and death.

Resurrection of the mortal body (2 Cor. 4:16–5:8)

For some modern theologians, the good we experience now is the realization of the promise of resurrection. Not so for Paul. The resurrection power of God not only revives and sustains us in our pain, as we serve others, but will be fully revealed only in the future when God raises our bodies to immortal life.

This is what 4:16–5:8 is all about. The movement of thought in this passage is similar to Philippians 3:10, 11: "I want to know Christ and the power of his resurrection and the sharing of his sufferings by becoming like him in his death, if somehow I may attain the resurrection from the dead." Conformity to Christ's death now, the experience of the power of Christ's resurrection now, and the future resurrection of the body—these are the main elements in this passage and in 2 Corinthians 4:7–5:8.

In 4:13-15 Paul says that he speaks in accord with his faith (4:13). This faith is a spiritual knowing that the day is coming when the God "who raised the Lord Jesus will raise us also with Jesus, and will bring us with you into his presence." Not only was resurrection power revealed in Paul's ministry (4:8-11) and in his converts (4:12) but that same power is going to raise both minister (imagine: a cracked pot can have an eternal inheritance!) and converts and bring them into the actual presence of God. As Paul said in 7:3, "We die together and live together."

In the day of final resurrection, God will vindicate the faith of Paul's converts and his ministry in bringing them to faith. Pastor and parishioners will triumph together! What an appeal to take him seriously and refuse the allegations of his opponents against him. Paul's togetherness with his converts on the sea of glass will leave no room for further complaints against him. In the light of what will be, why not stop the complaints now? This is the implication of Paul's words.

He ends the passage with the affirmation that everything he has done has been for the Corinthians, so that, beginning with them, an ever widening chorus of praise to God may result as more and more people come to experience what the Corinthians have experienced through the ministry of their servant Paul (4:15).

Once again, as in 2 Corinthians 4:1, Paul says, "We do not lose heart" (4:16). There is no flagging of zeal or giving up, not even if our outer nature (our mortal body) is wasting away, for our inner nature (the real person we are) is being renewed day by day (just as we are being transformed into the image of the Lord from one degree of glory to another— 3:18). This is all part of our preparation for what is to come in God's future (4:17). Paul's words in describing this are carefully chosen. He speaks of our "slight, momentary affliction." Corresponding to "slight" in the phrase following is "beyond all measure." Over against "momentary" stands "eternal," and transcending "affliction" is "weight of glory." Contemplating the eternal glory to come is what makes the present affliction both slight and momentary. We do not *feel* this way when we are going through trials, but faith in the crucified and risen Christ tells us it is so. We will need to remember this as we go through the "time of trouble."

Faith reveals that we should "look not at what can be seen [our afflictions] but at what cannot be seen [the glory of God's kingdom]; for what can be seen is temporary ['momentary,' 4:17], but what cannot be seen is eternal" (4:18). I try to remember this every time I visit the graves of my first wife, her parents, and my father. What I see there is temporary; what God has prepared for these dear ones and all of us is eternal. Thanks be unto God!

Paul realizes that the earthly tent (mortal body) he lives

in may not only waste away (4:16) but be destroyed, that is, die as a result of life's severity. But since we look not to what is seen but to what is unseen (4:18), we know that we have "a [new] building from God, a house not made with hands, eternal in the heavens" (5:1). Here Paul speaks of the resurrection body, which is part of the glorious age to come. In anticipation of this event, we groan, for we long to be clothed with our heavenly dwelling (5:2). The idea of groaning is found in a similar set of ideas in Romans 8. Here the creation groans (8:22) as it longs for freedom from bondage to decay (8:21); and we groan as we await the fullness of our adoption, the redemption of our body (8:23). Until that future time, God's Spirit groans with us, as it intercedes for us during periods of suffering and prayer. The same Spirit that shouts "Abba, Father" with us in the realization of our sonship (8:15) groans with us in our suffering (8:26). God knows our pain and is going to do something about it.

Paul would like the glory of the new age and resurrection body to overtake this age and body before he dies. He does not want to be found "naked" or unclothed (2 Cor. 5:3), which would be the situation after death since the old body disintegrates and the new body is not yet here until Christ comes. "Naked" refers to the death experience as being devoid of a body. Paul desires to avoid this state and have what is mortal swallowed up by life. The God who "is preparing us for an eternal weight of glory" (4:17) is preparing us for this immortal life. As a guarantee or first installment of this life he has given us the gift of the Spirit. As Romans 8:11 says: "If the Spirit of him who raised Jesus from the dead dwells in you, he . . . will give life to your mortal bodies also through his Spirit." The Spirit is the pledge and presence of eternal life.

As Paul has mentioned faith (2 Cor. 4:13) and knowing (4:14; 5:1), he now twice mentions confidence (5:6, 7). He is totally confident of the victory of the eternal over what is mortal. He realizes that while he is presently home in the body, he is away from the Lord. This is a relative, not absolute statement, for Paul knows that just as resurrection power now accompanies him (4:8-11), his transformation to glory is already taking place (3:18), and because the Spirit is already present as the first installment of the future (5:5), he is not really separated from the Lord. As a matter of fact, in Galatians 2:20 he says, "Christ lives in me." However, the veil that separates us from the full reality of knowing God, which involves being with God face to face, has not yet been torn aside (1 Cor. 13:12). Thus we now must walk by faith, not sight (2 Cor. 5:7). True enough, Paul wishes that the final and full vision of God and experience of being with God were already here. "We would rather," he says, "be away from the body and home with the Lord" (5:8). This cannot refer to a disembodied state, for Paul says he does not want to be found "naked" (5:3). Furthermore, his emphasis has been on resurrection (4:14). No, he is speaking about the day of final transformation and resurrection. It cannot come too soon.

This passage has affinity with Philippians 1:21-24. Here Paul says dying is gain, for it involves being with Christ, which is far better than anything else. He is pressed between his desire to be with Christ and the need to remain in the present life for the sake of the Philippians. Some have taken this as a reference to a disembodied state after death, just as they do the corresponding words in 2 Corinthians 5. Those who understand it thus think Paul is talking theologically here. Actually he is talking psychologically. The old warrior is tired. He has had too many battles and would like to go home to be with Christ whom he has served so long through such great difficulties. When Paul does speak theologically about being with Christ, he speaks only about resurrection, which he wishes to attain by becoming like Christ in his death (Phil. 3:10, 11) and for which he waits. As he says: "But our citizenship [commonwealth, KJV] is in heaven, and it is from there that we are expecting a Saviour, the Lord Jesus Christ. He will transform the body of our humiliation that it may be conformed to the body of his glory" (Phil. 3:20, 21).

Life in the interim (2 Cor. 5:9, 10)

Until Jesus comes to take us home with Him, Paul's one aim is to please the Lord (5:9), something the Corinthians and Paul's critics needed to know. We are to live for Him who died for us (5:14). And as Paul has emphasized that all of his present life is lived in the presence of God (2:17; 4:2), so in the future he, his converts, and his critics will stand before the judgment seat of Christ to receive from Him in accordance with how they have lived in the body. Have they lived to please God? This is *the* question. Let all who judge others take note.

Thus the section that began with his rivals' judgments upon him (4:1-5) ends with a statement of Christ's judgment upon them. In view of this judgment, our choice is between living to please Christ by loving others or living to please self by judging others. Which will it be?

*Reconciliation is at the same time a gift
and a summons,
a mercy and a command.*

Chapter 6

2 Corinthians 5:11–6:2

RECONCILING THE RECONCILED

What's going on here?

How do we visualize Paul writing his letters with the great themes they contain? The major subject of 2 Corinthians 5:11–6:2 (especially 5:14-21) is reconciliation. Do we suppose that one day Paul got the urge to write a general statement on the meaning of reconciliation and then later thought about who he might send it to and the purpose it might have for them? Do we write letters this way today, expressing ideas that have no particular context and then trying to fit our thoughts to some person or group?

I don't think so. A letter is not a treatise or essay. It is a personal communication written to a specific person or persons and having particular issues, questions, explanations, challenges, or requests in mind. Second Corinthians 5:11–6:2 is part of a very personal message. It has real theological substance, but it was written for a very practical purpose—one that met a real need in the Corinthian church and its relations with Paul.

An outstanding illustration of the practicality of a seemingly very theological passage is the great hymn of Christ's descent and ascent in Philippians 2:6-11. This passage, over which an incredible amount of theological debate has raged, is very practical in its purpose. It illustrates and inspires the conduct Paul desires of the Philippians: (1) unity in a shared mind of love; (2) humility rather than jealousy and

competitive strife; and (3) service to others (2:2-4). The theologically debated story of emptying Jesus in verses 6-8 illustrates these very traits and is told to stimulate a duplica-
tion of the mind of Jesus in believers.

Likewise in 2 Corinthians 5:14-21 we have marvelous theological affirmations whose purpose is to give insight and
bring change in the way the Corinthians evaluate Paul and
their own lives and spiritual experience. In this passage Paul
is trying to bring about a long-sought-after reconciliation
between himself and his converts. Their relationship has
been strained to the breaking point, and Paul wants to heal
the almost deadly wound.

How does a pastor go about the practical work of healing
fractured relationships? Not with a list of rules but with a
delineation of what God has done for us as the basis for how
we ought to treat each other. Second Corinthians 5:11–6:2
teaches that God has reconciled us to Himself and invites us
to receive this reconciliation and apply it to our personal
relationships. The world-reconciling activity of God was
called upon by Paul to heal the rift between himself and his
converts and, by extension, between all of us today.

A ministry of persuasion (2 Cor. 5:11-13)

Just preceding and introducing his focus on reconciliation, Paul declares that he is engaged in a ministry of persuasion (5:11). The kind of persuasion he speaks of has nothing to do with the devious deceptions of the high flying
orators so common in his day. Rather, it is done "knowing
the fear of the Lord." This phrase is connected with 5:10,
which speaks about the judgment. In view of God's final assize, Paul conducts himself with reverential fear and cir-
cumspection before God. He senses his accountability to God
and says in verse 12 that he is "well known to God." Just as
God can read the sincerity of his motives, he also hopes he is
known as a person of integrity to the Corinthians as well.

This ministry of persuasion is not the kind that attempts
to please people at any cost—a type Paul rejects in Galatians
1:10. Rather, in the fear of the Lord he seeks to persuade

people of the truth of the gospel, and in 2 Corinthians 5:11–6:2 that particularly means the truth of reconciliation with God.

Paul speaks about the kind of ministry he has, not to commend himself, but to give the Corinthians an opportunity to take pride in him (rather than to complain about him) and to "be able to answer those who boast in outward appearance and not in the heart" (5:12). It is obvious that boasting "in outward appearance" refers to his opponents and "in heart" refers to himself. Paul is not concerned about splashy presentations and flashy commendations but about the state of his heart before God.

And when it comes to the question of having an enthusiastic religious experience where the power of the Spirit was especially manifest—Paul calls it being "beside ourselves"—this is a private experience alone before God. Apparently, Paul's opponents contended that he publicly exhibited none of the outward manifestations of the Spirit and thus could not be a real apostle of God. His answer is that such manifestations are personal and private, not public. The real evidence of his apostleship is that he speaks in his right mind, without open displays of religious exuberance, so that the Corinthians may benefit thereby (5:13). This argument is similar to 1 Corinthians 14, where Paul says that though he speaks in tongues more than his converts, in church he would rather speak five words with his mind so as to instruct others than ten thousand words in a tongue (14:18, 19).

What Paul says, as he speaks with his mind, is of greatest benefit for his converts, because it is motivated by the love of Christ spoken of in 2 Corinthians 5:14. Paul's ministry and relations with the Corinthians were governed and guided by this love, not by blatant displays of religious enthusiasm. Let's look then, at verse 14.

One for all (2 Cor. 5:14)

What moves Paul forward in his ministry is the love of Christ. He says that this love "constrains" him (KJV). This means that it controls the course he takes; it inspires, activates, propels, and compels him to take only actions befitting the love of Christ. This is the motive force that "urges us on" (NRSV).

To live in accordance with this love, one must know the nature of it. So we ask: What is the content of this love? Paul answers simply: "One has died for all." The connection between the love of God and the Cross of Christ is strongly emphasized by Paul. If people want to know about God's love for them, all they have to do is look at the Cross. It is the proof of God's love (Rom. 5:5-8; 8:31-39; Gal. 2:20 speaks of the "Son of God who loved me and gave himself for me"). The statement in 2 Corinthians 5:14 that "One has died for all" was not a Pauline invention but the heart of Christian faith shared by Christians everywhere.

In 1 Corinthians 15:3, 4, Paul appeals to the earliest Christian confession we possess. It begins: "Christ died for our sins according to the Scriptures." The "our" of this text becomes the "all" of 2 Corinthians 5:14. The message of this "all" can be expressed in the words of three texts of the New Testament. According to 1 Timothy 2:4, 6, "[God] desires everyone to be saved . . ." and "Christ gave himself a ransom for all." In the thought of 1 John 2:2 Christ is "the atoning sacrifice for our sins, and not for ours only but also for the sins of the whole world." Hebrews 2:9 says that Christ tasted death for everyone. It would not accord with "He died for all" (2 Cor. 5:14) to say that He died for some, for the elect (thought of as a limited number), or for believers alone. Christ's death is universal in its range and significance. It is "in behalf of" the entire human race.

Since Christ died for all without exception, Paul teaches that all without exception have died in His representative death. This emphasis upon "all" does not say that all necessarily will be saved, for it is clear from the passage that God's reconciling appeal must be accepted (5:20), and His grace must not be rendered vain (6:2). God has given an awesome power to human beings—by faith to accept His grace or by rejection to frustrate it. We can say Yes or even No to Him who has said Yes to us (1:20). The ultimate, personal realization of salvation is contingent upon saying Yes. This does not make faith (our Yes to God) a cause of salvation but the means whereby we are personally attached to the only cause of salvation, Jesus Christ.

The death Jesus died was "for (*hyper*) all." What is the sense of the "for"? Its earliest and most essential meaning is "over." This took on the meaning of one bending over another to protect him. This idea may well lie behind the thought of Galatians 3:13: Christ redeemed us from the curse of the law by becoming a curse "over" us. Christ, as it were, bends over us, and the curse necessarily falls on Him instead of us.

Thus it is easy to see how "over" develops into the meanings associated with the concept of representation: "in behalf of," "for the benefit (sake) of," or "for." It may also carry a substitutionary sense: "in place of."

In 2 Corinthians 5:14 the primary sense seems to be representation: Christ's death is our death (just as our senator in the United States Senate represents us, and his or her vote is in effect our vote). That is why the text goes on to say, "Therefore all have died." However, in a secondary sense, substitution is present as well for, by virtue of Christ's death, none of us needs to personally experience the ultimate death ("the second death") that is sin's due.

New life, new evaluation, new creation (2 Cor. 5:15-17)

Verse 14 makes such an important affirmation that it could stand alone. In the context, however, its function is to provide the foundation for what Paul says in verse 15. Verse 15 is the destination to which verse 14 is traveling. Paul is the theologian of the Cross and Resurrection. In verse 14 he is moving from the Cross so as to arrive at the Resurrection in verse 15. The practical significance of verse 14 is to announce that Christ's death *for* all had as its purpose that we who live as a result of it should live no longer *for* ourselves but *for* Him who *for* our sake died and rose again. Verse 14 involves the principle of "one for all," and verse 15 stresses "all for one." Thus we who have received new life as a result of Christ's death are to conduct that life not in our own self-interest, as we did before being personally joined to Christ, but with Christ's interests in mind. Christ is to be the object of our affection, the goal of our living, and the inspiration and standard of our service.

This has outstanding relevance to the situation in Corinth, for Paul's correspondence reveals that the Corinthians were very self-centered, arrogant, and critical of others, especially him. Paul tells them that if they are taking their cue from Christ's death for them, which involves their death to the old ways and empowerment to a new, Christ-centered living, their relations to him and each other will be radically altered. This is why he says in verse 16 that we no longer regard anyone from a merely human point of view (Greek: "according to the flesh"). This even includes Christ Himself. Before the resurrection appearance of Christ to Paul, he saw Jesus as a failed messianic pretender who did not bring what Jews expected of the Messiah and who was out of harmony with the Torah, as his followers were. His encounter with the living Christ changed all that.

Thus the ways we used to think and judge people and life are gone as a result of the risen life of the crucified Christ flowing through us. Transformed perception rather than worldly perception is now to reign (cf Rom. 12:2: "Do not be conformed to this world, but be transformed by the renewing of your minds, so that you may discern what is the will of God—what is good and acceptable and perfect"). Paul is exhorting the Corinthians to see him and his work through the lenses of the "new creation" in Christ rather than with the old specs of the world. According to Galatians 6:14, 15, "the world has been crucified to me, and I to the world." As a result of this crucifixion, nothing that used to count counts anymore. All that matters is the new creation. This is the topic Paul moves on to in 2 Corinthians 5:17.

When Paul says in 5:17 "If anyone is *in Christ*," he is referring to a personal connection with Christ and not to something that is merely legally true. An examination of all the uses of "in Christ" in Paul's writings (164 occurrences) reveals that "in Christ" is to be understood more in terms of a marriage relationship than of a legal status arising from the decision of a law court, even God's court. It is an experiential reality referring to the most intimate union possible between the risen Christ and the believer. Because the believer is united with the living Lord through the indwelling of His Spirit, he or she is made a part of the saving events of Christ's death and resurrection and included in the body of Christ, the Church. As a result, the believer personally receives all the blessings of salvation that flow from Christ and exist in the fellowship of believers.

According to 5:17, when one is in Christ, it is not merely that he or she becomes a new creation but that he or she become part of God's new creation. The individual is included in a reality larger than himself or herself. The new creation, expected by Jews only at the end of time, is for Paul an already existent reality, created by God through Christ's death and resurrection. Personal access to this new creation comes only by union with the risen Christ. When entry to the new creation through this union takes place, everything old passes away and everything becomes new (5:17). This is another way of saying that in view of Christ's representative death for all, and the new life to be lived for Christ alone (5:15), we are no longer to judge anything from a worldly point of view (verse 16).

Those who belong to Christ are a totally changed people. They look at things and people the way Christ did because they have the mind of Christ (1 Cor. 2:16; Phil. 2:5). Husbands are to view their wives and wives their husbands with the mind of Christ and treat them as Christ would. Parents are to look upon their children and children their parents with the mind of Christ. Ministry should view laity through the filter of Christ's mind and laity the same with ministry. Physicians, dentists, nurses, and therapists should understand and treat their patients with Christ's spirit. Teachers should manifest Christ's mind with their students and students likewise with their teachers. And we should treat sinners, of whom we are all a part, with the healing compassion of Christ. We should treat the poor, defeated, and rejected with His mind; the disabled, divorced, and homosexuals with His mind; and different races, nationalities, and religious groups with His mind. If we do not manifest the healing, saving, restoring compassion and love of Christ in our evaluations of and relationships with others, then we are not really in Christ at all. To be in Him is to be and act like Him.

Reconciliation accomplished and applied (2 Cor. 5:18-20)

It is clear from verse 18 that the reconciliation of humanity to God has already been accomplished through Jesus Christ and that the ministry of this accomplished reconciliation has been entrusted to God's apostolic messengers, chief of whom is Paul. Since Paul is God's special agent of reconciliation (mentioned also in verses 19 and 20), the implication for the Corinthians is that they should give heed to God's message of reconciliation and His special appeal through His ambassador Paul. They are to allow themselves to be drawn into the reality of reconciliation that God has achieved by reconciling the entire world to Himself at the Cross.

It is because the realm of reconciliation already exists that the paradoxical call to let oneself be reconciled can be made. Without the objective reality there could be no subjective appropriation. But without personal acceptance, the objective reality cannot take effect for the individual. Salvation is not accomplished in a set of books or formulas but in the hearts and lives of people. In 2 Corinthians 5 there is no way around the interconnection between reconciliation as achieved by God and received by mankind.

"Be reconciled to the God who has reconciled you" is the paradoxical message of 2 Corinthians 5. Reconciliation is at the same time a gift and a summons, a mercy and a command. In the Corinthians' alienation from Paul, the very instrument of God's reconciling appeal, this truth was being lost sight of. To end suspicion and hostility and be on right terms with Paul, it was necessary for the Corinthians to more fully enter the domain of God's reconciliation. Somehow they were short of realizing the full potential of the Cross. Paul calls them to this.

An illustration of the same kind of thing is found in Ephesians 2:11-18. Here the alienated Gentiles have been brought near to the people of God by the blood of Christ. He embodies in Himself the peace that can exist between Jews and Gentiles. As their peace, He has broken down the dividing wall of hostility between them so that He might create in Himself one new humanity in place of two and reconcile both groups to God through the Cross. In consequence of this He has proclaimed peace to those both far off and those near. The text is clear. Peace is already objectively present; now it is to be experientially realized. The reality of peace and the proclamation inviting us to receive it go hand in hand. "Become what you are; realize in your lives what you already have in Christ"—this is the message. The gospel does not call us to a salvation that might be but to one that already is and that therefore impinges on our daily lives.

The great exchange (2 Cor. 5:21)

When Paul says in verse 21 that God made the sinless Christ to be sin for us, he is resurrecting the thought of verse 14 about Christ's death for us in a new and more striking form. Since the two statements are both talking about Christ's death for us, it is most likely that by "being made sin for us" Paul is talking about Christ as a sin offering; that is to say, one who bears our sins (verse 14). As verse 15 describes the intended result of verse 14, so the second half of 5:21 gives the intended result of the first half of the verse. Christ identified with us in our sins and bore them "that we might become the righteousness of God in him." To be the righteousness of God, in the context of a passage emphasizing the reconciliation that God effected and to which He invites us, is tantamount to saying "so that we might be reconciled to God in him."

Becoming the righteousness of God means that in being reconciled to God we begin to live for Christ in that His love propels us to serve others in love (verse 14). Becoming rightly

related to God, therefore, has very important implications
for establishing right relations with others, which is what
Paul seeks to foster through this passage on reconciliation.

The time of salvation is now (2 Cor. 6:1, 2)

In his capacity as a co-worker with God in the cause of
reconciliation, Paul now urges the Corinthians not to make
God's grace vain (6:1). How could they do that? By not living
in reconciliation with others after having learned the good
news that God has reconciled them to Himself through Christ
(5:18) and has forgiven all their trespasses (5:19). If they do
not live in forgiveness toward and reconciliation with
others after receiving their reconciliation to God, they short-
change the full meaning of reconciliation and frustrate its
purpose to change their lives.

Therefore Paul says, in accordance with Isaiah 49:8, that
the acceptable time, the day of salvation, is here (just as the
new creation is here—5:17). This is a remarkable statement.
The reconciliation already made at the Cross is now said to
be present as something to be accepted. In effect Paul says:
"Get off your high horses and make a decision to let God's
reconciliation determine your conduct and relationships,
especially with me."

Paul's thought reminds us of the message of Hebrews in
which, though God's rest is already present, the readers are
enjoined: "Today if you hear his voice, do not harden your
hearts" (Heb. 4:7). The salvation won yesterday at Christ's
cross is an event that turns the eons from yesterday to today. It makes all time Today. And thus it can be said: "But
exhort one another every day as long as it is called 'today,' so
that none of you may be hardened by the deceitfulness of
sin. For we have become partners of Christ, if only we hold
our first confidence firm to the end" (Heb. 3:13, 14).

What we all need to understand is the paradox that what
by God's grace alone is already finished is not yet finished
until it is finished in our lives. Not legal adjustments but
personal transformation is God's goal for our lives.

*Servanthood to God is the real issue,
and Paul's commendation derives not from words
but from what he has faced in his service for Christ.*

Chapter 7

2 Corinthians 6:3-13

HARDSHIP AND VIRTUE

It has been said that the best way to persuade people about something is to argue from your own life. Paul is still trying to bring about a full reconciliation between himself and his converts in Corinth. What better way to do that than to show what he has gone through as an apostle and how he has conducted himself through hard times. He believes that if the Corinthians really see the cost of his discipleship and the integrity of his character in tough times, they will be won to him, who won them for Christ.

As he begins his litany of suffering and rectitude, he tells the Corinthians that it has been his constant purpose to avoid any offense that would call into question the character of his ministry (2 Cor. 6:3). He is not so much concerned for himself as for the office he holds by divine commission. There is a stumbling block in the gospel—that salvation comes through an implement of suffering and shame (1 Cor. 1:23)—but the life of the minister should contain nothing that would cause anyone to stumble. A servant of God must exercise extreme care and caution, so that the ministry entrusted to him or her will be revered and not reproached. A pastor's words and life should correspond. Preaching and practice should harmonize. What was true of Christ should be true of the minister. "Not only did He teach the truth, but He was the truth. It was this that gave His teaching, power" (*Education*, 79).

Paul's concern was directed to this very goal. He now points to his sacrificial past to aid the cause of reconciliation in the present.

True ministerial credentials

Paul did not believe in self-commendation, as his heady opponents did, but could say: "As *servants* of God we have commended ourselves in every way" (6:4). Servanthood to God is the real issue, and his commendation derives not from words but from what he has faced in his service for Christ. It is written in the experiences of his life as an apostle. His life speaks for itself.

When people apply for university positions, they are asked to submit a Curriculum Vitae (CV), a synopsis of their background, education, professional experience, and published writings. Everyone tries to make their CV as impressive as possible. Search committees and administrative leaders seriously study these descriptions of exploits accomplished and positions held. I wonder what job Paul would be hired for based on his CV? Here's a look at his record.

Hardships (2 Cor. 6:3-5)

Paul does not first list his education or degrees, though testimony elsewhere indicates he was at the head of his class (Gal. 1:14). Surprisingly, he presents a list of his hardships. There are three categories of these and three types of difficulty in each category.

The first category includes "afflictions, hardships, and calamities." "Afflictions" comes from the Greek word *thlipsis*, whose underlying meaning is "pressing" or "pressure." Pressures that weigh down a person can come from inside one's own spirit or from other people and circumstances. In 2 Corinthians 7:5 Paul says that he was "afflicted in every way—disputes without and fears within."

The second word, "hardships," comes from the Greek *ananke,* which basically refers to something that is a necessity, and hence, in our text, to a hardship that cannot be avoided. To be a missionary, as Paul was, is to meet up with distresses one cannot run from. "Calamities" derives from *stenochoria*, which literally means "narrowness." Life can be filled with narrow, suffocating straits with no way of escape.

The second category has to do with distressful situations imposed by others. There are "beatings, imprisonments, and riots." Paul certainly knew about these, for they occurred frequently in his experience. In 2 Corinthians 11:23 he speaks of "far more imprisonments, with countless floggings, and often near death." He can even identify how many times some of these things happened: floggings—five times; beaten with rods—three times; stoning—one time (11:24, 25).

The third category deals with elements of experience that in a sense were self-imposed: "Labors, sleepless nights, and hunger." These three difficulties are closely related. Paul's "labors" probably refer to his hard work in various places in order to earn enough money to keep himself going while he toiled as a missionary and minister. Even though he had a right to financial help (1 Cor. 9:4-14), he had resolved not to accept any assistance from the Corinthians (9:15-17; 2 Cor. 11:7-11; 12:14-18). He did this in order to make his gospel of God's free grace free of charge (1 Cor. 9:18). Thus, to meet the needs of living and evangelizing, he had to work, undoubtedly at night as well as during the day. The best time for evangelism would be in the evening when workers were home. Because he didn't always make enough money from tent making or other forms of work, he sometimes went hungry, and perhaps, when he was working very hard in evangelism, he may not have had time to eat.

Paul did not list these struggles with a "poor me" attitude, to show what a martyr he was. To be sure, he desired sympathy and concern from the Corinthians, but his main burden was for them to recognize him as a man of patient endurance. Before beginning his list of hardships, he says that his commendation relates not merely to his trials but to the great endurance he manifested as he underwent affliction (2 Cor. 6:4). This is what carried him through.

"Endurance" comes from the Greek word *hypomone*, which

literally means "remaining under." It refers to that stubborn and strong quality of character that makes it possible for a person to bear trial without giving way. It is like a fortress that cannot be taken. It is a very praiseworthy word in Paul's vocabulary of virtue. In 1 Corinthians 13 it is the climactic characteristic of love (13:7)—love not only believes and hopes all things but also bears and *endures* all things. In a related idea, it "never fails" (13:8). Using a corresponding word (*makrothumia*), patience (or longsuffering in the KJV) is also love's first characteristic. In a number of New Testament lists of virtues, patience sits side by side with love (1 Thess. 1:3; 1 Tim. 6:11; 2 Tim. 3:10; Titus 2:2).

What gave Paul the fortitude to stick out his trials except his love for his spiritual children? What gave Mother Teresa her staying power through wearying labor and painful circumstances if not her love for the poor and dying?

Thus patient endurance under fire shows character, and this is what Paul wanted the Corinthians to see about himself. This major thought prepares the way for the list of virtues he presents as being part of his life, virtues that continue to operate and remain intact even under trial.

Virtues (2 Cor. 6:6, 7)

In addition to steadfastness under trial, Paul manifested a number of other traits that were part of his commendation as a servant of God (6:4). These included "purity, knowledge, patience, kindness, holiness of spirit, genuine love, truthful speech, and the power of God" (6:6,7). There is a close link between the first three of these characteristics and the Holy Spirit. Knowledge is one of the Spirit's gifts (1 Cor. 12:8), and patience and kindness are among the fruits of the Spirit (Gal. 5:22). As far as Paul is concerned, such gifts are received from God, not achieved by mankind.

The word for patience used here (*makrothumia*) means that spirit of longsuffering that endures hurts inflicted by others without being provoked to return evil for evil. Instead of giving back in kind, it gives "kindness" instead. The Greek word for "kindness" has the idea of graciousness in it. Instead of reacting to wrong harshly, the Christian acts graciously. The qualities of "patience" and "kindness" are the two leading characteristics in the depiction of love in 1 Corinthians 13:4-7.

The next of these virtues translates as "holiness of spirit," referring to the human spirit. It is the trait of character called for in 2 Corinthians 6:17 and 7:1. This trait is accompanied by "genuine love." The association between holiness and love is beautifully illustrated in 1 Thessalonians 3:12, 13. Here Paul is engaged in prayer for his converts, and he prays that the Lord will make them abound in love *so that* their hearts will be unblamable in holiness at Jesus' second coming. Love, according to this text, is the content of holiness.

However, it is possible to translate the word *spirit* in 2 Corinthians 6:6 not as a reference to the human spirit but the Holy Spirit. In this case the Spirit of God would be the driving force behind "genuine love" (as it is the initiator of the fruit of love in Gal. 5:22).

Two further traits are "truthful speech" and "the power of God." As holiness of spirit (or the Holy Spirit) is connected with love, so truthful speech and the power of God may go together. It is God's power that makes possible Paul's speaking the truth. This answers his critics who charged him with using veiled or misleading speech.

Interestingly, the phrase "truthful speech" can be rendered by "word of truth." As such it may be a reference to the gospel, which is sometimes called the word of truth (Eph. 1:13; Col. 1:5). According to this understanding, Paul would be saying that the gospel is made effective by the power of God. In this regard we may recall Romans 1:16: "I am not ashamed of the gospel, for it is the power of God."

Armaments and reputation (2 Cor. 6:7, 8)

The third category of Paul's CV has to do with spiritual warfare and reputation. Paul declares that, in addition to his virtues during times of hardship, he is armed with the weapons of righteousness for the right hand and the left. He enjoys military metaphors and here employs them to say that, in terms of the weapons that righteousness supplies for use in its service, he is fully equipped for battle. He has offensive weapons for the right hand and defensive weaponry, the shield, for the left. Thus he has been equipped to accomplish the task set forth in 2 Corinthians 10:4, 5: "To destroy strongholds . . . arguments and every proud obstacle raised up against the knowledge of God, and we take every thought captive to obey Christ."

This full equipment for spiritual battle, while impressive and promising, does not mean that God's wielder of the sword will be liked. No, he must act "in honor and dishonor, in ill repute and good repute" 6:8).

Paradoxical status (2 Cor. 6:8-10)

Paul's CV moves on to the paradoxical status of his life as God's servant. In a moving series of antithetical statements similar to 1 Corinthians 4:12, 13, he describes, on the one hand, what he has endured and on the other, what the truth about himself really is. The negative side shows his status in the eyes of the world; the positive how his situation is to be viewed "in Christ." As he taught, when a person is "in Christ" nothing looks or is the same any longer (2 Cor. 5:16, 17). Paul presents seven antitheses that illustrate this.

Antithesis 1: **"We are treated as impostors, and yet are true" (6:8).** Since in their estimation Paul lacked proper letters of recommendation, his critics called him an impostor. The word *impostor* comes from a Greek verb meaning "to wander." Paul was accused of being a wandering masquerader who deceived others about his status. Against this notion of embodying falsehood stands Paul's conviction that he is true—meaning true to God, true to his commission, true to the gospel, and true to his converts.

Antithesis 2: **[We are treated] "as unknown, and yet are well known" (6:9).** Those super-apostles who were super critics of Paul accused him of being a no account; one who had no official standing whatever. But many of his converts knew him well and some even said, "I belong to Paul" (1 Cor. 1:12). Beyond these, he was fully known by God, in whose service he worked.

Antitheses 3 and 4: **[We are treated]** *"as dying, and see—we are alive, punished, and yet not killed" (2 Cor. 6:9).* This refers to the many afflictions, persecutions, and near-death experiences Paul had. Danger accompanied him daily; the prospect of death was his constant companion. This recalls 4:10, 11, where he says that he always carries in his body the death of Jesus and is "always being given up to death for Jesus' sake." However, when it looks like he is down and out, he lives! "Struck down, but not destroyed" describes his experience (4:9). Resurrection power is at work in him in the midst of his suffering. He counts on God, who raises the dead. He rescued him in the past and will rescue him in the future (1:9, 10).

Antithesis 5: **[We are treated]** *"as sorrowful, yet always rejoicing" (6:10).* As Paul observed the powers of opposition and criticism arrayed against him and his ministry, he could not help but sorrow. Yet he rejoiced because he knew nothing could ultimately thwart God's plan or separate His people from Him. Hear him in another letter written a little later from the city of Corinth:

> Who will separate us from the love of Christ? Will hardship, or distress, or persecution, or famine, or nakedness, or peril, or sword? . . . No, in all these things we are more than conquerors through him who loved us. For I am convinced that neither death, nor life, nor angels, nor rulers, nor things present, nor things to come, nor powers, nor height, nor depth, nor anything else in all creation, will be able to separate us from the love of God in Christ Jesus our Lord (Rom. 8:35, 37-39).

Antithesis 6: **[We are treated]** *"as poor, yet making many rich" (2 Cor. 6:10).* Here Paul's life imitates His Master who was rich, yet for our sakes became poor so that through His poverty we might become rich (2 Cor. 8:9). Paul was actually poor but, by proclaiming Jesus as Saviour, he made many rich.

Antithesis 7: [*We are treated*] *"as having nothing, yet possessing everything" (6:10)*. This emphasizes and gives a new twist to the preceding line. Though materially poor, he brought spiritual riches to others, but he himself is also spiritually rich. Though outwardly possessing nothing, on the spiritual level he possesses everything (see 1 Cor. 4:21, 22). A relationship with Christ brings God into one's life and enriches every aspect of existence. With Him we possess everything.

A plea for affection (2 Cor. 6:11-13)

Isn't it interesting? Paul says he possesses everything, and yet there is one thing he still desires—the heartfelt affection of his converts. It is as with his Lord—Jesus has everything and yet covets our love. God loves us so much that He wants our love back (Deut. 6:5). It is the nature of love that it seeks reciprocity. One-sided love has a tragic dimension.

Great leaders of the church may be well-known for their love. However, it may seem that they dwell in a kind of sacred isolation, needing nothing in return. Nothing could be further from the truth. Pastors, teachers, and administrators need our love. It is fuel for their tired, self-giving souls.

So Paul says: "Our mouth is open to you, Corinthians" (2 Cor. 6:11, RSV). By this Paul means that he has spoken to them freely and candidly. And, as he has hidden nothing concerning himself, so he does not want to hide the fact that his heart is open wide to them. There is plenty of room for all of his converts in his heart, and that's just where he wants them (see 7:3: "You are in our hearts"). So all-encompassing is his love for them that he says affectionately and yearningly, "You are not restricted by us, but you are restricted in your own affections" (6:12, RSV). There were no limits on Paul's love for them, but he felt they had reservations about their love for him.

Paul feels somewhat like a jilted lover. His love is intact, but he yearns for the affection of his beloved "in return" (6:13). Here again is the motif of reciprocity. It is not that

Paul, like a businessman, wants a return on his investment; but like a spiritual father he wants the full fellowship, confidence, and love of his family. Thus he makes the plea, "Open wide your hearts also" (6:13), which means the same thing as, "Make room in your hearts for us" (7:2).

If Paul felt this way toward his recalcitrant converts, how must God feel toward us? He has prepared a place for us in His home (John 14:2). The question is, Will we make a place for Him in the home of our hearts? (14:23). Jesus stands at the door and knocks. If any of us, no matter who we are or what we have done, will open the door, He will come in and eat together with us in the fellowship of an eternal union (Rev. 3:20).

The Christian church is founded upon the righteousness of God as that which produces righteousness in His people.

Chapter 8

2 Corinthians 6:14–7:16

PURITY AND PENITENCE

Sidetracked or on track?

Have you ever had the experience of talking or writing on a particular topic when all of a sudden another pressing thought enters your mind and you abruptly switch gears to give vent to the new thought? This thought forms a digression after which you return to your original subject. As a teacher, I have done this many times. However, there are occasions when I cannot return so easily to my original theme. At such times, with a bit of humor, I may ask my students, "What was I talking about?" They are always very happy to get the forgetful professor on track again!

Second Corinthians 6:14–7:1, with its talk about holiness and separation from the world of unbelievers, seems very much like a digression, for in 7:2 Paul continues the subject he was on in 6:11-13. The last statement in these verses is "Open wide your hearts also" (6:13). The first words of 7:2 are "Make room in your hearts for us." In between is the section on separation, which seems to break the theme Paul has been pursuing. So different is this topic that some have thought an editor of Paul's letters may have inserted 6:14–7:1, a part of other Pauline writings, in this spot. It has even been suggested that these verses belonged to a letter preceding 1 Corinthians, mentioned in 1 Corinthians 5:9. This does not seem to be the case, for that letter admonishes against dealings with immoral people within the church

(1 Cor. 5:10), and 2 Corinthians 6:14–7:1 deals with unbelievers outside the church.

The question is: Why is this passage located right where it is found? It is conceivable that at 6:13 Paul stopped dictating his letter to do something else, and when he returned, another major thought was pressing on his mind that he wanted to deal with before returning to his theme in 7:2. If this is what happened, then 6:14–7:1 would have no necessary connection with the context. It would be a true blue digression.

However, as we read the content of this passage in the light of Paul's interests in the larger context, I believe we can discover why Paul put this passage just where he did. He was not sidetracked at all.

Paul's driving concern was reconciliation between himself and his critical converts. He wanted to be in their hearts as they were in his. What would it take to have a real heart-to-heart relationship with each other, where there could be mutual respect and love? For Paul the answer was clear. The Corinthians, who had let cultural concepts and customs influence their understanding of the Christian gospel and life, had to change.

Paul's letters to Corinth are shot through with evidence that for his converts the world influenced the gospel more than the gospel influenced their understanding of the world. This was a major problem Paul was trying to remedy. How could there ever be meaningful heart fellowship if those Paul was trying to keep from the world kept going back to it for their presuppositions, values, and style of life?

Real reconciliation and fellowship could only take place if Paul's heart and theirs were on the same wavelength. So when Paul says, "Make room in your hearts for us [me]" in 7:2, just after the supposed digression, he means more than just wanting them to like him. Rather, he desires them to take him *and all he stands for* into their affections.

A young man is reputed to have asked his girlfriend's father for her hand in marriage. The father sternly replied, "You'll take her all or nothing!" That is what Paul wanted—

for them to take him entirely into their hearts and lives. Fellowship with Paul would have to be based upon the reality underlying his life and summarized in Galatians 6:14: "May I never boast of anything except the cross of our Lord Jesus Christ, by which *the world has been crucified to me, and I to the world*" (emphasis supplied). Were the Corinthians prepared to experience the same crucifixion and truly obey Paul's injunction to be separate from the world? (2 Cor. 6:17).

As a man and woman can marry and live in harmony only if there is agreement between them in their essential values, so reconciliation and fellowship between Paul and his converts could only happen if they were willing to be separate from the world, belong exclusively to Christ, and live under the insignia of the Cross.

The temple of the Living God (2 Cor. 6:14–7:1)

In 1 Corinthians 3:16 Paul had raised a question that is pertinent to 2 Corinthians 6:14–7:1: "Do you not know that you are God's temple and that God's Spirit dwells in you?" Paul here calls the church a temple indwelt by the Holy Spirit. This is precisely what he was trying to get the Corinthians to recognize in 2 Corinthians 6:14–7:1. The Greek word for "church" (*ekklesia*) literally means "the called out." The words *sanctification* or *saint* (both built on the same root) refer to God's setting apart something or someone to belong to Him and to be enlisted in His service.

The words *church*, *sanctified*, and *saints* occur together in 1 Corinthians 1:2. Thus, at the very beginning of the Corinthian correspondence the believers in Corinth were identified as "the called out" and "the set apart." Now in 2 Corinthians 6 Paul wants them to make good on this divinely initiated reality in their daily lives.

He introduces his remarks by a pointed command: "Do not be mismatched by unbelievers" (6:14). Paul is not talking about a potential danger but one that already existed. The Greek form he employs means "Stop being mismatched with unbelievers." The Corinthians had never completely left the world, and Paul enjoins them to end those former allegiances and partnerships that might compromise their new Christian stance.

The word *mismatched* is the translation of a phrase that literally means "Do not be yoked together with another of a different kind." The idea of yoking is taken from the field of animal husbandry and recalls Leviticus 19:19, which enjoins the Israelites not to let their cattle breed with others of a different kind. The same thought is also found in Deuteronomy 22:10, where it talks about not plowing with an ox and donkey yoked together.

In this injunction against mismatching, Paul is not primarily talking about marriage but about various kinds of contaminating relationships between Christians and non-Christians. Not all contact can be avoided, of course (see 1 Cor. 5:10), but to have the kind of intimate association that might lead believers to be involved with what is "unclean" (2 Cor. 6:17) must be avoided. Regular concourse with unbelievers would be a real mismatch, for the outlook of the two groups is so drastically different.

Just how different is seen in the list of rhetorical questions Paul now introduces to support his point about separation. He first asks, "What partnership is there between righteousness and lawlessness?" (6:14). Paul knew better than to suppose all righteousness was in the church and all lawlessness without. First Corinthians gives plenty of evidence that lawlessness, to a greater extent than one might imagine, was in the church. However, the Christian church is founded upon the righteousness of God as that which produces righteousness in His people. This righteousness stands unalterably opposed to lawlessness, which is a characteristic of the world (see 1 Cor. 6:9, 10; Rom. 6:19 describes the pre-Christian state of his readers to be that of ever-increasing lawlessness—2 Cor. 4:3).

In the questions that follow, Paul asks how such antithetical principles as light and darkness can fellowship with each other; how Christ can be in accord with Belial (another name for Satan); how one who believes in Jesus Christ can have a part with one who has no faith in Him;

and how God's temple could be in agreement with the idols belonging to heathen temples (2 Cor. 7:14-16). This last question reflects the problem seen in 1 Corinthians 8:10 of a believer in a pagan temple eating food dedicated to the heathen deities represented by idols. As Paul says in 1 Corinthians 10:20: "What pagans sacrifice, they sacrifice to demons and not to God. I do not want you to be partners with demons." He then goes on to show the total incompatibility between eating the Lord's Supper and partaking of the table of demons.

In all these questions, the words Paul uses for connection with that which is the opposite of Christian faith show that Paul is not talking about casual contact with the pagan world but intimate, participatory conduct. Notice how these words, a different Greek term for each question, are translated in the Revised Standard Version: *Partnership* and *fellowship* (2 Cor. 6:14); *accord* and *in common* (6:15); and *agreement* (6:16). These words suggest not only being in the world but playing with the world and finding unity with it. The implication of Paul's instructions is clear: Avoid all such relationships.

Paul then quotes some Old Testament promises and one command that are relevant to the church as "the temple of the living God" (6:16). Quoting from memory, he gives a free rendition of each Old Testament text but declares that God said all of it (6:17). Here are the promises and the command.

Promise
I will live in them and walk among them,
and will be their God
and they shall be my people (Lev. 26:12 and Ezek. 37:27).

Command
Therefore come out from them
and be separate from them, says the Lord,
and touch nothing unclean (Isa. 52:11).

Promise
Then I will welcome you (Ezek. 20:34)
and I will be your father,
and you shall be my sons and daughters,
says the Lord Almighty (2 Sam. 7:14).

The command stands in the center of the promises, and paradoxically, is both the result of the promises and the condition for their fulfillment. Because God is the God of grace who promises His presence among us, He asks His people to separate from the world so as to fellowship with Him. Obedience to this command is the presupposition for the mutuality of a father/child relationship (2 Cor. 6:18).

From this Paul draws a concluding appeal: "Since we have these promises, beloved, let us cleanse ourselves from every defilement of body and spirit, making holiness perfect in the fear of God" (7:1).

The command to cleanse oneself from all defilement (7:1) is a reformulation of the command to be separate and touch nothing unclean (6:17). To speak of "body and spirit" is not to talk about two parts of a person but about the totality of one's being. As we cleanse ourselves in response to God and in the power of His grace, we move closer and closer to that perfect holiness, which accords with reverence for God. Holiness is the issue, as God said to Israel in a statement containing similar elements to 2 Corinthians 6:16 and 7:1: "For I am the Lord your God; sanctify yourselves therefore, and be holy, for I am holy. You shall not defile yourselves" (Lev. 11:44). Believers are called to remain unstained by the world (James 1:27).

Renewed appeal (2 Cor. 7:2-4)
Corinthian partnerships with the world had been crowding out fellowship with Paul. Having admonished them to withdraw from worldly associations, Paul now returns to the theme of heart reception and says: "Make room in your hearts for us" (7:2). Then, instead of speaking further about those alliances with the world that would dissipate fellow-

ship with himself, he once again summarizes the charges against himself that could derail the process of reconciliation if they were true. He hastens to assure the Corinthians that he has wronged no one, corrupted no one, and taken advantage of (defrauded) no one. His denial could not be more emphatic. The fact that Paul once again disavows the charges against him shows just how pervasive and strong they were.

He then tells them that rehashing their criticisms was not meant to heap condemnation upon them. Rather, they have such a secure place in his heart that he dies and lives together with them (2 Cor. 7:3); meaning, come what may, whether death or life, thick or thin, he is with them in affection.

This reminds me of the wedding vows I sometimes administer. The couple's commitment is: "For better or worse, for richer or poorer, in sickness and health, to love and to cherish, until death do us part." Paul does one better. He does not say to live and to die together but follows to die by to live. Perhaps there is a hint here of the resurrection power of God lifting the Corinthians to a richer spiritual life in their reconciliation with Paul after their negative death-dealing criticism of him.

Especially in view of the success of Titus with the Corinthians, which he is about to describe, he says happily: "I often boast about you; I have great pride in you; I am filled with consolation; I am overjoyed in all our affliction" (7:4).

The "God who consoles the downcast" (7:6) spoke consolation to Paul through Titus. As Paul heard of the Corinthians' longing, mourning, and zeal for him, his joy overflowed (7:6, 7). Then he remembers the grief his severe letter caused them. He is sorry for that yet happy about it, for their grief led them to repent by making a new appraisal of Paul and finally dealing with the offender mentioned in 2:5. Being a "godly grief," he feels that in the long run they really weren't harmed by the painful things he wrote in his letter (7:8, 9).

In fact, says Paul, there are two types of grief. There is

the godly grief that "produces a repentance that leads to salvation and brings no regret." This is the grief the Corinthians experienced. Their repentance saved the day with Paul and affected their ultimate salvation.

There is no doubt about it—repentance, a turning to the Lord (or, in this case, the Lord's agent, Paul) and a turning away from wrong is a prerequisite for salvation. We are not saved by our works, but God's grace works repentance, and repentance bears fruit for salvation. And when one turns to the Saviour and away from sin, there is no regret.

But there is another kind of grief. This is worldly grief, and its fruit is death. This kind of grief, instead of leading to repentance and rectification of wrong, turns in on itself in self-pity and rises no higher than the self's concerns. It neither focuses upon the person hurt nor responds with a changed behavior that would make things right. In caring for no one but self and harboring ill will, resentment, and bitterness, it injures itself.

On another level, worldly grief can simply be the pain of being caught in wrong, not pain over the wrong itself. (See *Steps to Christ*, pages 23-25 for excellent comments on this.) This kind of grief bears no fruit for salvation but leaves one in death.

In 2 Corinthians 7:11 Paul turns to the evidence that the Corinthians have repented toward him. He notes their *earnestness* to make things right, their *eagerness* to clear themselves of misunderstandings as to how they handled the matter of the person who offended Paul (2:5), their *indignation* over the wrong done to Paul, their *alarm* over the possibility of a rupture in their relationship with him, their *longing* and *zeal* to solve the matter, and the actual *punishment* they administered (7:11). Repentance is not a head trip. It decisively deals with the problems that need to be solved.

Paul's conclusion is that they ultimately have proved themselves guiltless in the matter (7:11). He also says that the primary focus of his sorrowful letter was not the injurer or the one injured "but in order that your zeal for us might be made known to you before God." In other words, an important purpose of Paul's letter for them was that, through what it stirred up in them, they might become conscious of the fact that their zeal for him outweighed their criticism (7:12). On his side, it was to let them know of his abundant love for them (2:4). Paul found comfort in the fact that this is what actually happened (7:13).

Joy abounding (2 Cor. 7:13-16)

Paul not only felt good himself from the report Titus brought, but his joy was enhanced by the fact that Titus also had his anxious mind set at rest by the Corinthians (7:13). Paul had recommended Titus to them and them to Titus, and Paul's confidence in both had proved legitimate (7:14). Titus's heart had gone out to the Corinthians because they obeyed Paul and greeted him with due regard for his commission by Paul.

Paul ends the chapter by saying that he has "complete confidence" in his Corinthian converts. This caps off Paul's argument in chapter 7 and diplomatically prepares the way for the major offering he will solicit from the Corinthians in chapters 8 and 9.

The note of joy throughout 2 Corinthians 7 (verses 4, 7, 9, 13, 16) needs to be captured and applied. Life may get rough, charges may abound, afflictions may multiply, and relationships may be threatened. But above and beyond, and yet within the circumference of our struggles, we find the "God who consoles the downcast" (7:6). He can bring new joy out of the ashes of our pain, new attitudes out of old criticisms, repentance out of recalcitrance, comfort out of discomfort, and confidence out of mistrust. This is because He is "the God who raises the dead" and "who rescued us" and "will continue to rescue us" (1:9, 10).

*Our perception of the needs of others will rise
in direct proportion to our recognition of
God's incredible grace to us.*

Chapter 9

2 Corinthians 8 and 9

A MINISTRY
OF GIVING

The mother of all offerings

Grousing sometimes accompanies the taking of church offerings. "The church is always after my money" is heard all
too often among Christians. However, without money the
church cannot sustain its life; fund its missionaries, evangelists, and pastors; support education; build churches; or,
above all, minister to those in need. The love of money is the
root of all evil (1 Tim. 6:10), but the availability and use of
money for both sustenance and advance is absolutely necessary.

It is a little-known fact that one of the most important
aspects of Paul's ministry, one that engaged him for years,
was the collection of an offering from Gentile Christians to
aid the poor Jewish Christians of Jerusalem. So significant
was this offering gathered from the churches of Galatia,
Macedonia, and Achaia that we could term it "The Mother
of All Offerings" (patterned after the term "The Mother of
All Battles," used during the battle over Kuwait in 1991).

The success of this offering could lead to a unified Christian church; its failure to a fractured church, divided between Jewish and Gentile Christians. Furthermore, the delivery of this offering to the Judean Christians would legiti-
mize Paul's apostolic calling in their eyes. As for Corinth,
the offering would test their obedience to Paul's authority
and gospel—the gospel that says we are all one in Christ

(Gal. 3:28). Also, with the completion of this project, Paul would be able to turn his attention from the eastern Mediterranean, where he had been working so long, and go to Rome as he had dreamed for years, then from Rome on to Spain, the western edge of the Roman Empire. This would be the final frontier of his missionary work. There never was a more important offering in the history of the Christian church.

Read all about it

Not having heard much about this offering before, some may wonder if Scripture places much emphasis upon it. Indeed it does. A precursor of this offering is found in Acts 11:27-30. When a large-scale famine took place during the reign of Claudius, as the prophet Agabus had predicted, the church of Antioch decided to send whatever relief they could to the believers in Judea. Barnabas and Saul were bearers of the offering. Paul's interest in the welfare of the Judean Christians grew over the years, and in Acts 24:17 we hear him say, "Now after some years I came to bring alms to my nation."

The origin, nature, and purpose of this offering, so briefly alluded to by Luke, are spelled out in Paul's letters. The earliest reference is Galatians 2:1-10. As part of a major conference in Jerusalem called to decide whether Gentile believers should be circumcised so as to be in unity with Jewish believers, it was requested of Paul, the apostle to the Gentiles, that he remember the poor Jewish Christians. Paul responded that this was something he already had been eager to do (2:10).

His eagerness was translated into concrete deeds, as we see in 1 Corinthians 16:1-4. This passage contains directions for taking up offerings for the Jerusalem project. This was one of the issues the Corinthians had raised in their letter to Paul mentioned in 1 Corinthians 7:1 (compare with 16:1). Paul had asked them to contribute, and they wanted clarification on how it should be done.

First Corinthians 16:1-4 gives the necessary details. Paul

is very diplomatic in his response. He assures the Corinthians, some of whom wondered about the legitimacy of the offering (see 2 Cor. 8:21), that it was part of a joint enterprise. The Galatian churches were also contributing, and the directions given to them should be followed by the Corinthians as well. On the first day of each week, each believer was to put aside and save at home (the text says nothing about Sunday offerings in church) whatever extra they had earned. This money should be ready when Paul and his associates made a pastoral call to collect it. As a guarantee that the offering would reach its destination, the delivery would be made by those appointed by the Corinthian church with letters of recommendation. Paul would go as well if it seemed advisable.

A year went by and the Corinthians had not yet done anything toward the offering (2 Cor. 8:10; 9:2), probably because of their troubled relations with Paul. Paul wrote 2 Corinthians 8 and 9 to urge the Corinthians to get on the ball and complete what they had promised to do. He gives them strong motivation by reminding them of what Christ had done for them and that their gifts would glorify God and He would bless them.

The rationale for the offering is given in Romans 15:25-29. As Paul writes his letter to Rome, he is in Corinth, about to leave for Jerusalem with the offering. What might be advisable (1 Cor. 10:4) has now become actual: He personally is going with the others to deliver the offering. The issue involved in the offering—unity between Jewish and Gentile Christians—had become so urgent that he had to be directly involved, despite the fact that he was putting his life on the line with the unbelieving Jews, who could assassinate him because they believed he was teaching contrary to Jewish tradition.

In appealing to the Romans to contribute, Paul uses diplomacy by explaining why the churches of Macedonia, Achaia, and Corinth were donating: "Macedonia and Achaia have been pleased to share their resources with the poor among the saints of Jerusalem . . . and indeed they owe it to them; for if the Gentiles have come to share in their spiritual blessings, they ought also be of service to them in material things" (Rom. 15:26, 27).

This passage contains a very important point for Christians. We have not always treated our Jewish brothers and sisters well. We fault them for not accepting Jesus as the Messiah and for connecting righteousness with works. Each of these points is worthy of study, but notwithstanding its shortcomings, Judaism with many of its teachings and love of God's law has been a source of spiritual blessing for the Gentile world (Rom. 15:17). Though the nonbelieving Jews need enlightenment, they do have a zeal for God (Rom. 10:2), "and to them belong the adoption, the glory, the covenants, the giving of the law, the worship, and the promises; to them belong the patriarchs, and from them, according to the flesh, comes the Messiah" (Rom. 9:4, 5). If through them, even in their stumbling, riches have come to the world, how much more will their full inclusion in God's final people mean! This is Paul's prophetic dictum in Romans 11:12.

Thus, as Paul believed that a Gentile contribution to Jewish welfare was the thankful payment of a huge debt to spiritual forebears, might not the same recognition be meaningful and relevant today? Money cannot do everything, but helping needy Jews might testify that Jesus' followers are filled with a saving love, and thus Jesus might be seen as who He really is, the Saviour of all mankind.

Characteristics of a fund-raiser

1. *Leadership.* To raise funds for an important cause, someone has to assume leadership. There needs to be a catalyst, a central organizing force. It has been said that "everybody's business is nobody's business." Though tired from overwork and oppressed by conflict, Paul took up the task of leadership, found associates to work with him, and did all he could to raise funds for the poor.

2. *Diplomacy.* Paul was skilled in knowing how to frame an offering appeal. When he wrote to the Romans, hoping they would aid him morally and financially in his projected

evangelistic work in Spain, he waited fifteen chapters before telling them that he was going to Spain and needed their help. He first concentrated on the well-known faith of the Roman church (Rom. 1:8), and how deeply he desired to see them to bring them a spiritual gift and do evangelism among them (1:9-15). Throughout the book he gives them a thorough understanding of his gospel message of God's righteousness creating one new people out of Jews and Gentiles and how this gospel can help them solve practical problems in their lives together (1:16–15:13). Only after this does he tell them his evangelistic plans beyond Rome and ask for their support in sending him on his way (15:24). Paul was a diplomat indeed.

In 2 Corinthians, just before two whole chapters devoted to the Jerusalem offering (chapters 8 and 9), he assures them that they are his pride and joy and that he has complete confidence in them (7:4, 16). This sounds a long way from his rebuttal of all the criticisms they had made of him and his attempts to forge reconciliation with them (1:12–7:2). Furthermore, he lets them know that they have such a place in his heart that he is ready to face anything with them, whether death or life, or as we say today, "come hell or high water" (7:3). He also lets them know he is sending Titus back to them to bring the collection to completion (8:6). This is the same Titus who so appreciated their compliance with Paul's directives and their respectful welcome on his last visit (7:15). There is a real hint here that they should continue to heed Paul and welcome Titus with open arms again as he attempts to get the job done. Unquestionably, Paul has prepared well for his offering appeals in 2 Corinthians 8 and 9.

3. *Honesty*. Paul made his intentions clear: "We intend that no one should blame us about this generous gift that we are administering, for we intend to do what is right not only in the Lord's sight but also in the sight of others" (2 Cor. 8:20, 21). Honesty requires openness and guarantees to givers that their gifts will reach the goal and be used correctly. This is all the more the case when, as with Paul, skep-

tics would be all too glad to find a flaw and punch a hole in the effort. Every good cause has opposition. So Paul decided that the funds would be superintended not by himself alone but by a group whose qualifications he gives (8:16-24). Titus is mentioned as well as two unnamed brothers, the first a famous gospel preacher and the second a tested person who had tremendous eagerness about the offering because of his great confidence in the Corinthians. Here were people the Corinthians could connect with and have confidence in. This committee would function as auditors. A fund-raiser's claim of accountability only to God should never be allowed to be a smoke screen for misuse. The church must see how funds are being handled. "In God's sight and your sight" should be the rule.

4. *Psychology.* A fund-raiser has to know how to appeal to people's minds and hearts. For example, Paul knew how to use complementarity and comparison to advance the offering. He spotlighted the Corinthian virtues: faith, knowledge, and love (2 Cor. 8:7) in order to say "Make your generosity equal to your other traits." How could one have love but not generosity?

Paul also drew comparisons with other churches to stimulate mutual interest in the project. In 8:1-4 he uses Macedonia (probably thinking in particular of the Philippians) to give incentive to the Corinthians of Achaia. Paul's description of the Macedonians is very moving. He says that although they were undergoing an intense affliction, they did not focus on their trouble but maintained their joy in the Lord, "and their extreme poverty overflowed in a wealth of generosity" (8:2).

How can poverty be generous? It can't afford it! But when you don't have much yet give all you can, that is a "wealth of generosity." When someone does this, it is not only giving according to one's means but beyond one's means (8:3), because one's own interests are placed in jeopardy for the sake of sharing with others even more destitute.

In order to help the Corinthians see what a generous spirit really is, Paul says that the Macedonians not only did not need to be asked but begged earnestly for the privilege of sharing in this ministry of giving (8:4). This had to be a stimulus to the Corinthians, for they were much better off than their counterparts in Macedonia. Macedonia and Greece were longstanding political rivals. Paul now gives the Corinthians an opportunity to continue their rivalry in a meaningful cause—the rivalry of goodness!

Interestingly enough, Paul could flip the coin the other way and use the Achaians to motivate the Macedonians! He had boasted to them about the eagerness of the Corinthians of Achaia to be involved (9:2). He told them that Achaia had been ready for a year, and this picture of zeal really stirred up the Macedonians (9:3). Then Paul skillfully turned the tables again and said that if the Macedonians came with Paul to Corinth and found them not ready, there would be humiliation for all (9:4).

Motivations for giving

There can be false motives for giving, such as to avoid guilt, to replace personal involvement in service, and to receive human praise, as in Matthew 6:2. Motivations God seeks are of a totally different sort. Beyond those implied above in Paul's use of complementarity (excellence in virtue must include generosity) and comparison (don't lag behind other Christians), the apostle supplied profound motivations for Christian giving.

1. *The gift of God.* Sometimes the last word a person speaks is the most important word spoken. I think that is the way it is with 2 Corinthians 9:15. Paul exclaims: "Thanks be to God for his indescribable gift." This paean of praise directed to God immediately follows a statement beamed right at the Corinthians. Paul speaks of "the surpassing grace of God that he has given you" (9:14). Our perception of the needs of others will rise in direct proportion to our recognition of God's incredible grace to us. We could rephrase Jesus' statement on love to say: "Give to one another as I have given to you" (John 15:12).

The accent on grace is not only found at the very end of this section but at the beginning as well. Paul says God's grace is something we need to know about and that it has been granted to the churches of Macedonia (2 Cor. 8:1). When the text then goes on to describe the extent of their giving (8:2, 3), we realize Paul wants us to understand that behind every gracious gift to others stands the supreme Giver. What else could account for their activity but the grace of God inspiring them? If we keep our focus on God, we will not be able to forget the needs of others. This means that giving is tied not primarily to commands but to the heart of the gospel. That is what the next point is all about.

2. *The example of Christ.* In a most moving statement it is said of Jesus: "For you know the grace of our Lord Jesus Christ, that though he was rich, yet for your sake he became poor, so that by his poverty you might become rich" (8:9, RSV). This is the great exchange. Christ takes what we have, and we get what He had. This text is related to Philippians 2:6-8, which describes Christ as inhabiting the majesty of heaven and being equal with God, yet exchanging His divine form for human form and the throne of God for the wood of the cross. The exchange that Christ made in our behalf is expressed with reverential beauty by Ellen White:

> Christ was treated as we deserve, that we might be treated as He deserves. He was condemned for our sins, in which He had no share, that we might be justified by His righteousness, in which we had no share. He suffered the death which was ours, that we might receive the life which was His (*The Desire of Ages*, 25).

She further says:

> Whether rich or poor, we must never forget that the poverty of Christ was a part of His legacy in humanity. It was not alone His betrayal in the garden or His agony upon the cross that constituted the atonement. The humiliation of which His poverty formed a part was included in His great sacrifice (*SDA Bible Commentary*, 6:1103).

Again, Christ's identification with the poor is emphasized:

> The Son of God had left His heavenly home, with
> its riches and honor and glory . . . not to live in the
> palaces of kings, without care or labor, and to be
> supplied with all the conveniences which human
> nature naturally craves. In the councils of heaven
> He had chosen to stand in the ranks of the poor
> and oppressed, to take His part with the humble
> workers. . . .
> The world never saw its Lord wealthy *SDA Bible
> Commentary,* 6:1103, 1104).

If Christ could identify with the spiritually and physically
poor, cannot we, the recipients of His grace, do so as well?

3. *A demonstration of our love.* Deriving directly from the
two points above, as God's gift is an evidence of His love for
us, so our gifts give dynamic proof of our love for others. It is
one thing to acknowledge that what God has done for us is
the basis for what we do, but it is another thing to actualize
His love toward others in everyday life. It is too easy for
right belief to take the place of right action. Profession and
practice are two different things. If we say we love, we must
demonstrate it before human beings. Paul tells the
Corinthians: "Therefore openly before the churches, show
them [the messengers from the churches, 8:23] the proof of
your love and of our reason for boasting in you" (2 Cor. 8:24).

In the parable of the unmerciful servant, the man who
was forgiven a ten-thousand-talent debt by the king was
expected to forgive those who were debtors to him. He did
not, and the judgment of God consigned him to everlasting
loss—so seriously does God expect that His love to us will be
passed on (Matt. 18:23-35). In like manner, 1 John combats
the philosophy that a mere assertion of love for God avails
in the eyes of God, without love for others. John insists that
the knowledge that we have passed from death to life re-
sides in the fact that we love one another (1 John 3:14). God's
love is known by the fact that He laid down His life for us,

and we should do the same (John 3:16). In practical terms, John asks how God's love could ever be said to abide in one who had worldly goods but refused to help someone in need (3:17). His conclusion is that we should love, "not in word or speech, but in truth and action" (3:18).

I once saw a truly beautiful enactment of love. My father had a massive heart attack while visiting his homeland of Croatia. I got there in time to spend his last days with him. While I was there, I greatly desired to visit a staff member of the United States embassy in Zagreb with whom I had talked by phone about my father's condition before I left for Croatia. The gentleness of her speech and her extremely caring attitude, not only for my father but also for me, had made a deep impression on my mind.

I met her soon after my arrival, and a few days later she called me to the embassy. She said she had been thinking about our situation, and this was what she was impressed to do. Without asking me if I had sufficient funds but knowing that it would cost thousands of dollars to take my father back to the States after he breathed his last, she offered to loan me her savings in the bank—all her savings. What she said burned its way into my heart and mind forever: "Mr. Blazen, I wish to do this, not for your sake primarily but the sake of our Lord Jesus Christ who has done so much for us. And I do this not to win His favor but only to express gratitude for the favor He already has done for us." She was, for Jesus' sake, about to hand over her entire life's savings to a stranger. I was able to take care of the expenses myself, but I shall never forget this kind Catholic lady who dramatically exemplified the love of Christ in action.

4. *A fair balance*. Paul saw all believers as members of one body (1 Cor. 12:12, 13). Because this was so, he believed that a fair balance should exist between abundance and need. In urging the Corinthians to give, Paul did

> not mean that there should be relief for others and pressure on you, but it is a question of a fair balance between your present abundance and their need, so

that their abundance may be for your need. . . . As it
is written [Exod. 16:18], "The one who had much did
not have too much, and the one who had little did
not have too little" (2 Cor. 8:13-15).

The abundance the Corinthians enjoyed could help the
poor Christians of Jerusalem, and one day they might be
able to help the Corinthians in a time of need. In fact, as
Romans 15:25-29 states, the Gentiles have already reaped
rich blessings from the Jewish people. The old principle is
valid once again: "One for all, and all for one."

5. *Sowing and reaping.* Paul points to a principle of agri-
culture: "The one who sows sparingly will also reap sparingly, and the one who sows bountifully will also reap bountifully" (2 Cor. 9:6). The point is that when you are bountiful
in attempting to meet the needs of others, you need not worry
about your own needs, for "God is able to provide you with
every blessing in abundance, so that by always having
enough of everything, you may share abundantly in every
good work" (9: 8). Contrary to ordinary self-centered understanding, Paul's formula is this: Giving does not create short-
ages but abundance. This is because God richly blesses givers (9:8).

In addition, part of the blessing of giving is its connection
with righteousness. What is true of God, that in giving to
the poor His righteousness endures forever (9:9), will be true
of those who follow God's example. "He who supplies seed to
the sower and bread for food will supply and multiply your
seed for sowing and increase the harvest of your righteousness. You will be enriched in every way" (9:10, 11). It is a
righteous thing to give!

We should not, however, conceive of giving as a business
investment but as spiritual enrichment. As we follow God,
He blesses our lives.

The nature of giving

Second Corinthians 8 and 9 are very clear about the spirit
in which giving should take place. First, there should be no

reluctance in giving (9:7), but it should be accompanied by eagerness. It is striking how many times this idea occurs (8:7, 11, 12, 16, 17, 22; 9:22). The great example is the Macedonians begging to give (8:4). Maybe in light of this we should not speak of *taking* offerings but only of *giving* offerings!

Second, if we are eager to give, it would be expected that we would cheerfully give. In fact "God loves a cheerful giver" (9:7). This leads logically to a third point, which is that we should give generously, another frequent idea (8:2, 6, 7, 9, 19, 20; 9:11, 13). If God loves a cheerful giver, He certainly must love a generous giver. Generosity includes self-sacrifice, and this is the heart of the gospel itself.

In the fourth place, that we give and how much we give must be a matter of personal decision. "Each of you must give as you have made up your mind." This goes with a fifth point, that no compulsion should be placed upon people to give (9:7). It is to be voluntary, not an extortion (9:5). Paul gives the best example of this principle because, though he so earnestly desired the Corinthians' contribution, he says to them: "I do not say this as a command" (8:8); and "I am giving my advice" (8:10). Sixth, we are to give in accordance with what we have, not in accord with what we do not have (8:12). Pressure should not be exerted for pledges that go beyond one's means.

A seventh consideration is that givers should fulfill their pledges and not leave the goal undone (8:6, 11). Persistence is a characteristic of true giving. If something is worth doing, the proverb says, it is worth doing well, and that includes the idea of finishing the task. Dropout givers do not bless the church, and Jesus did not commend the son who said he would do what his father asked but ended up not doing it. It would have been much better to have said he wouldn't, as did another son, and then to have done it after all (Matt. 21:28-31). Best of all is to say Yes and prove it to the end by deeds. The model for this is God, of whom it is said (to a church that really followed through with aid for Paul and others): "I am sure that he who began a good work in you will complete it at the day of Jesus Christ" (Phil. 1:6).

Finally, it is not just what we give but who we give that counts. Of the exemplary Macedonians Paul says: "They gave themselves first to the Lord and, by the will of God, to us" (2 Cor. 8:5). Before we consecrate our gifts, we are to consecrate ourselves to God and model this before His servants. Ellen White admonishes us: "Consecrate yourself to God in the morning; make this your very first work" (*Steps to Christ*, 70).

Results of giving

The most immediate benefit of giving is that it helps to supply the needs of the saints (9:12), but it does more than that. It enriches those who give (9:11), shows their commitment to the gospel of Christ (9:13) and, at its highest reach, glorifies God (8:19; 9:13) and produces an overflow of thanksgiving to Him, as expressed in: "Thanks be to God for His indescribable gift." When all is said and done, it is God who is to be praised, not man.

*If we wish to capture every thought of others
for Christ, we must first make sure all
our thoughts are captive to Him.*

Chapter 10

2 Corinthians 10

CAPTIVE TO CHRIST

A radical mood swing

We who read Paul's writings, especially a personal letter like 2 Corinthians, where Paul is up against the wall struggling for his apostolic life, need to be prepared for sudden shifts of mood, tone and emphasis, and even seemingly contradictory statements. A good illustration of a complete reversal of mood is found in Paul's letter to the church of Philippi. In the first two chapters Paul has been very positive, and his accent has been on joy. This reaches its climax in 3:1: "Finally my brothers and sisters, rejoice in the Lord." Then without warning, there is a profound change from the high of joy to the depth of danger: "Beware of the dogs, beware of the evil workers" (3:2).

Second Corinthians 10 to 13 has this same feeling compared to the reconciliatory tone of chapter 7 with its thankfulness for the Corinthians' renewed interest in Paul, its emphasis on their repentant spirit, and Paul's statement of "complete confidence" in them (7:16). Following this are two chapters on the collection for Jerusalem that accent the virtues of the Corinthians (8:7) and the virtues of God's surpassing grace shown them in His indescribable gift (9:14, 15).

It sounds like the Corinthian church has come to peace with its apostle and will now, through its generous offerings, contribute to peace between Jewish and Gentile Christians. Wonderful! We are therefore unprepared for the sudden change in the next four chapters. Here we find struggle and caustic comment against those opposing Paul's commission and authority. Day has turned into night, and the conciliator of chapters 1–9 has turned into the contender of chapters 10–13. From his opening statement in chapter 10, gentle encouragement is exchanged for biting sarcasm and angry threats. As the argument of chapters 10–13 unfolds, the bragging Paul earlier shunned gives way to a spiritual braggadocio that seems to have no limits. What has happened?

Some have suggested that chapters 10–13 belong to the severe letter Paul wrote between 1 and 2 Corinthians (2:1-4; 7:8), and were later added to the end of 2 Corinthians by an editor of Paul's inspired writings. As Ellen White's writings on different occasions have been collected into compilations, so it is thought that 2 Corinthians may be a mini-compilation.

Others believe that chapters 10–13 are from a separate letter written some time later when the situation in the church changed again due to the powerful influence of a group of outside intruders whom Paul calls "false apostles" (11:13).

However, as one reads 2 Corinthians, several indicators reveal that these false apostles did not come on the scene after 2 Corinthians 1–9 were written but were already operating in the church while Paul was composing these chapters. They are the peddlers of God's Word (2:17) who had letters of recommendation (3:1). With their strong Jewish background (11:22) they had placed emphasis on the prominence of Moses and the law, which is why Paul discusses this in 2 Corinthians 3. Further, Paul's denial of using shameful ways or tampering with God's Word (4:2) and his strong assertions that he had not corrupted or defrauded anyone (7:2) presuppose that the super critics, who were guilty of the very things they charged him with, were at work against him.

If the false apostles were already at work among his converts, why didn't Paul name them earlier in 2 Corinthians rather than waiting until the last chapters? This may be due to a rhetorical strategy used in Paul's day, wherein you only allude to the most difficult problem or people early in a discourse and then, at the end, really expose them and let them have it. The great philosopher Aristotle taught that this kind of discourse should include defense of oneself and blame for one's opponent at the end. This is what we find in the last four chapters of 2 Corinthians. Second Corinthians, then, would be a single letter that, in harmony with conventions of the day, reserved the nub of the problem and the ultimate blow against it for the last.

One thing is for sure: These "false apostles" had entered the church with high claims for themselves and a great disclaimer of Paul as a genuine apostle. Unfortunately, as time went on and the influence of Paul's opponents grew stronger, the Corinthians, already in some measure reconciled with Paul, began to have second thoughts about his authority and to accede to the intruders' estimate of him and the different gospel they preached. Chaos always threatens, and the work of God's servants is never finished.

Meekness and battle (2 Cor. 10:1-6)

If Ellen White, charismatic leader and authority that she was, were alive and began a talk to a church congregation with the words "I myself, Ellen White, appeal to you," the congregation would know that something very personal and important was up and that she planned to speak with authority on it. A person just does not name themselves unless the issue is very serious and the appeal strong. That's the way Paul begins chapter 10. He has concerns that he wants to address with his authority as an apostle of Christ. Thus he invokes his own name and uses the word *myself*.

Instead of a command or charge, he makes an appeal, an earnest entreaty based on the meekness and gentleness of Christ. He approaches his readers in the spirit of the incarnate Christ, who was "meek and lowly in heart" (Matt. 11:29). Even when dealing with strong antagonists and demeaning persons, our appeal must not be on their level but must reflect the character of our Lord. Interestingly, the term translated "gentleness" has the sense of forbearance, the opposite of vindictiveness. It is the patient endurance of abuse. Paul had plenty of abuse but determined not to act as his critics did.

They had accused him of being humble, a term that was used to characterize Jesus (Matt. 11:29) but was not seen as a virtue in the Greco-Roman Empire. They claimed Paul was "meek and mild," weak and abject, when he was with them but a bully when he was away writing letters to them and did not have to face up to them. In other words, tough on paper but timid in person; courageous when away but cowardly when present. In fact, they asserted that "his letters are strong, but his bodily presence is weak, and his speech contemptible" (2 Cor. 10:10). They thought he was nothing but a weak-kneed, poor mouthed preacher, lacking impressive bearing and polished speech.

Undoubtedly it was because of this charge of boldness and harshness in his letters that Paul says, "I appeal to you by the meekness and gentleness of Christ." He denies the charge and declares that he wants to talk in the spirit of Christ. However, how would you feel if someone made these charges against you? You might plan to speak in a Christian spirit but be overcome by memory of the slams against you and end up going strongly on the attack. This is what happened to Paul. He announces that, while the intent of his letters was not to frighten (10:9), his critics should understand that what he says in his letter he will also do when present (10:11).

However, he asks that he not be forced to be bold when he is present to deal with his opposition (10:2). He may not be able to avoid this, however, when thinking about the further charge that he acted on the level of mere human standards (the Greek literally means "according to the flesh"). Judging by the critics, Paul was such a lowlife he could hardly get off the ground into the higher realm of meaning, value, charismatic experience, and leadership. The inference of the critics was that, unlike Paul, they operated on the level of the Spirit, for they had a wisdom from beyond and spiritual experiences of the highest sort (implied in Paul's argument in 12:1-4).

This puts Paul in a fighting mood. Yes, indeed, he does live in the human realm (the realm of flesh), but he does not fight according to worldly (fleshly) standards. Paul's words suddenly thrust us into the realm of battle. He wants his enemies to know that he is willing to take them on, but his weapons are an altogether different sort than those ordinarily used. They are not human or fleshly at all. Here he does not tell us what these are, but we may surmise that they include the weaponry described in Ephesians 6:13-17, where he admonishes his readers to take up the whole armor of God. This includes "the belt of truth," "the breastplate of righteousness," the shoes of "the gospel of peace," "the shield of faith," and "the helmet of salvation."

However, whereas the weapons of Ephesians 6 are to be used mostly for defense—to withstand attacks of the devil—here Paul is thinking of weapons of offense, for he describes what they can do to overcome the enemy. He says that his weaponry gives him divine power, which his opposers thought he lacked.

The first thing this power could do is to "destroy strongholds." Ancient cities contained fortified towers, built to be impregnable if the city walls were breached. Paul sees his enemies as cloistered safe and secure in their bastions of defense, feeling invincible. But he who, like an army on pillage, could overrun and overturn the ground of the early Christians (the word *destroy* in Gal. 1:13 suggests this), could now by divine power not only breach the walls of his enemies' city but also attack their citadel and turn it into rubble, no matter what they hurled at him from above.

This doesn't sound like the spirit of the meek and gentle Jesus any longer, does it? But after all, even the gentle Jesus could turn ropes into whips, overturn the tables of the moneychangers, and throw them out of the temple. And we today who like to emphasize love and mercy can sing "Onward Christian soldiers, marching as to war."

What these metaphorical strongholds are is indicated by

the next sentence. "We destroy arguments and every proud obstacle raised up against the knowledge of God" (2 Cor. 10:4, 5). No matter what the arguments of his opponents are, the divine power that works in him can effectively refute them and knock down any resistance to the true knowledge of God. The battle against his gospel and attempt to take away his converts and alter their understanding of God will fail.

Not only can Paul destroy strongholds but his divine weapons will enable him to take captives of the enemy and make every thought obedient to Christ (10:5). This is something needed not only by those who oppose the gospel but also by us who have accepted it. Rebellious thoughts need to be subdued, and good thoughts need to be expanded and ennobled. Every thought should belong to Jesus and honor Him. The more we reflect on the good news, the more this will happen. What Paul said to the Philippians is relevant here: "Finally, beloved, whatever is true, whatever is honorable, whatever is just, whatever is pure, whatever is pleasing, whatever is commendable, if there is any excellence and if there is anything worthy of praise, think about these things" (Phil. 4:8).

Paul's warfare capability contained one other element. In contrast to the power to take every thought captive to *obey* Christ is the ability to punish every *disobedience* (2 Cor. 10:6). As he says in 13:2, if he comes again he will not be lenient, as he was on his painful visit. There is something he needs, however, to make disciplinary action possible. He says he is ready to punish disobedience when the obedience of the congregation as a whole is complete (10:6). Apparently there has been a large-scale turnabout from him, and Paul needs his congregation to come to their senses and yield to his authority once more. When they do, it will be easier to deal with those who remain rebellious. In a certain sense, when dealing with discipline, Paul's hands are tied until the congregation who needs to vote for and carry out the discipline is in toe again. His message in 10:6 is "Come back to me, and we will rout every disobedience."

Christian identity and authority (2 Cor. 10:7-11)

One of the hardest things to deal with is people who claim Christianity for themselves but deny it for others. They set up their own standard and judge everyone else in that light. This spiritual haughtiness does not befit Christians. Paul is astounded. In verse 7 he says in effect, "Take a good look at the situation and make a just call. You are confident that you belong to Christ, right? Well then, remind yourself of this—so do I! After all, I'm the one who brought you to Christ!" (see 10:14). It is clear that his rivals had gone so far as to say that Paul wasn't even a Christian, which was a low blow indeed for one who had given his whole life to Christ and His service. They said this of the one who asserted "For me to live is Christ" (Phil. 1:21). Incredible! What do you do with people who deny the very essence and meaning of your life? You survive them. As Robert Schuller of the Crystal Cathedral says in the title of one of his books, *Tough Times Never Last, Tough People Do*.

Paul goes on to admit that possibly he emphasizes his authority a bit too much, but he is not ashamed of that. After all, he says, it was the Lord who gave him this authority for the best possible cause: to build up the Corinthians, not to tear them down! (2 Cor. 10:8, compare 13:19). So even if he—this weak man with poor speech!—had to write a stern letter to them, its purpose was positive. It was for their good and not merely to induce fright (10:9, 10). His critics should remember, however, that his authority is such that it could frighten them if he comes to Corinth again (10:11).

Jurisdiction in ministry (2 Cor. 10:12-18)

Are there territorial spheres of ministry, some legitimate and others illegitimate? Paul certainly thought so. Just as his adversaries had contested his Christianity and ability, apostleship and authority, they also contested his ministerial jurisdiction. They felt they had the right—undoubtedly the duty—to work in the very territory he worked and with the very converts he made because their jurisdiction of authority and ministry not only overlapped but superseded his.

In verse 12 he ironically says that he wouldn't dream of classifying or comparing himself with his competitors who were in the habit of commending themselves. They seemed to have a spirit of competition, constantly vying with each other for top billing; all claiming to be the greatest.

To Paul's statement that he did not want to resort to the tactics of the self-commenders and self-comparers, who ultimately were comparing themselves with him, we can only retort: "Like fun you don't!" In no time flat Paul will feel compelled to compare himself on a grand scale with the opposition. He really doesn't believe in doing this, but they force him to it (see 12:11).

Paul is a real human being with real feelings trying to win a battle against endless charges and fears. His apparent inconsistencies can be chalked up to usage of different rhetorical devices and changes in his state of mind. We have to allow Paul, as inspired as he was, the same alterations of temper, approach, and argumentation that we ourselves use when embattled, upset, and concerned.

Paul charges his adversaries with lacking good sense when they compare and measure themselves with each other. But the issue goes deeper than that—they do not have a proper set of limits in their missionary endeavors. Paul's missionary policy was not to evangelize in areas where Christ had already been named and converts won. He refused to build on someone else's foundation (Rom. 15:20). So, with regard to bringing the gospel to the Corinthians, he was keeping within the field God had assigned him by reaching the unreached. He was the first to come all the way to them and had overstepped no boundaries and encroached upon no one else's labors (2 Cor. 10:13-15). In this way he was holding true to not boasting beyond the limits God had set. He could rejoice over his own converts, but he was not going to rejoice by involving himself with someone else's converts.

Paul's policy was to consolidate and enlarge his sphere of action among those he was already working for, and then, when their faith came to a sufficient degree of maturity, to move out from them to lands not yet explored for Christ

(10:16). By operating this way he would not be "boasting of work already done in someone else's sphere of action" (10:16). Only in this way could his own dictum, "let him who boasts, boast in the Lord," be fulfilled (10:17). When you boast in the Lord, you hold to the field the Lord has assigned you. When you work in someone else's territory, you are really boasting in yourself, not in the Lord. The implication cannot be missed: The rivals of Paul were completely exceeding their boundaries by entering into his territory and trying to win his converts for themselves. Paul's verdict in verse 18 is that they do this, obviously, to be able to commend themselves: "Look at us, we've got Paul's converts in our pocket now. No matter, for he is nothing, but we are really something." Paul says such a human judgment will not work, for "it is not those who commend themselves that are approved, but those whom the Lord commends" (10:18).

What we can learn

This chapter, while so deeply personal and argumentative, can teach us some important lessons for today.

First, we need to make our appeals in the spirit of meekness and gentleness when dealing with problems and antagonists. Paul may seem to have come short of this, but the principle he articulated and really tried to follow remains valid for us.

Second, we need the courage to be frank and to confront wrong. Evil acts—and so must we—with even greater energy.

Third, the power of darkness will attempt to destroy our reputations so as to destroy our work, conquer our converts, and divide our churches. We need to pray for and rely upon God's power to keep this from happening.

Fourth, we need to be aggressive, not merely defensive in relation to evil. We need to study Scripture and consult with one another for inspiration and understanding on how to demolish the strongholds of false argumentation that would keep people from a true knowledge of God.

Fifth, if we wish to capture every thought of others for

Christ, we must first make sure all *our* thoughts are captive to Him. I have a book with the title *Physician, Heal Thyself*. That gives the right idea for each of us. We have to be Christ's if we expect to win others to Him.

Sixth, we need to stop making comparisons with each other, trying to gain the upper hand in influence and power. The Lord is the One we need to compare ourselves with. When we do, we will discover that we come short and need His power to be present in our weakness.

Seventh, we need to exercise proper church discipline by dealing with every disobedience (10:6) that ruins the church's witness to Christ. Toleration of truly destructive persons can never be allowed.

Will evil be defeated, or will it win?
The stakes are high; a battle is raging.

Chapter 11

2 Corinthians 11

SUPER-APOSTLES AND SUFFERING APOSTLE

Deplorable methods

It is a very concerned and disquieted apostle who writes 2 Corinthians 11. He is much more concerned about his converts than about himself. But he has to talk about himself in order to deal with them, for they are suspicious of him. He is their anchor, and if the ship of the church is detached from him, it will be subjected to the greatest peril.

To get the Corinthians' attention, to warn them of danger, and to take them under his wing again, Paul resorts to methods of argument he thoroughly deplores. He is no fool, but he says he is going to speak like one. He is against boasting, except in the Lord, yet he is going to boast—really boast! He doesn't believe in comparisons with others, but he is going to make them. He doesn't like letters of recommendation, but he is going to talk a lot about his credentials. He wishes to speak with the meekness and gentleness of Christ, but he is going to roar against his opponents. Like the man in Romans 7, what he hates is what he does. But if by this tomfoolery, egotistical approach and vitriolic description of his adversaries he can grab the Corinthians from their clutches, he will resort to such means.

If someone were about to unknowingly step over a precipice, we would shout and holler, scream and yell! If someone were discrediting our education, experience, commitment and values, we would say things about ourselves that might embarrass us at any other time.

Danger of deception and domination (2 Cor. 11:1-6, 20, 21)

Paul begs his readers to put up with him in a little foolishness (11:1; of the twelve occurrences of this idea in Paul, eight are found in 2 Corinthians 10–13 and three in 1 Corinthians). His words are pure irony, for what he says is anything but foolish. He says that he feels a divine jealousy for them. This goes beyond a merely human jealousy over the fact that his converts are jilting him. The situation is much more serious that that. He is thinking of his converts from the point of view of God. The God of Sinai announces that He is a jealous God (Exod. 20:5), for He wants His people for Himself, not for the gods of this world. Paul says that, as a matter of fact, he is the Corinthians' spiritual father. Fathers plan marriages, and he has promised his betrothed converts as a chaste virgin to be joined to one husband, Christ (2 Cor. 11:2). But this chastity (which it was the Jewish father's duty to guard between betrothal and entry of the wife into her husband's home), is in jeopardy. Paul fears that instead of the marriage taking place they will be led astray as Eve was deceived by the serpent. Their minds will be corrupted by error, their spiritual virginity lost, and they will be deflected from a totally committed and pure devotion to Christ (11:2-5).

In chapter 10 Paul talked about divine power enabling him to take every thought captive to Christ (10:5), and yet here he is worrying that the thoughts of his converts will be led astray by others! Will evil be defeated, or will it win? The stakes are high; a battle is raging. God (and Paul) never promised that taking thoughts captive to Christ would be easy. It is not so much an event but a process, with the result achieved only through struggle.

Why does Paul think his people may fail to stay pure and endanger their marriage commitment to Christ? Because of those who have turned up proclaiming a different Jesus and different gospel than he proclaimed. Further, they offered a different Spirit than the one the Corinthians had originally received. These people are seducers posing as suitors. Unbelievably, Paul's very own spiritual children "submit to it readily enough" (11:4).

One thing is for sure—there was no way the adversaries of Paul could know Jesus as he did. Paul had met the real Jesus, now resurrected, on the Damascus road. They couldn't compete with Paul's personal knowledge.

There is told the story of a group of people meeting together one evening who decided that everyone would recite some literary piece. One of the speakers was a well-known actor whose gifted oratory and dramatic flair made possible an outstanding rendition of the twenty-third psalm. There was great applause.

Following the orator was a quiet man who likewise began to recite the famous psalm. Laughter greeted his inauspicious beginning. However, by the time he had gone through the entire psalm, the room was filled with a reverential silence that no applause could match. In a gracious gesture of recognition, the actor confessed to the man: "Sir, I know the psalm, but you know the shepherd" (William Barclay, *The Letters to the Corinthians*, 276). Unlike his accusers, who may have known something about Jesus, Paul knew Jesus himself and what the good news about Jesus really was. He personally had been transformed by his encounter with the risen Jesus.

When we think of the Corinthians' interest in the new teachings of these invading missionaries, it reminds us of Paul's speech at Athens. "All the Athenians and the foreigners living there would spend their time in nothing but telling or hearing something new" (Acts 17:21). The Corinthians, despite their Christianity, must have been something like this. When the new apostles with their claims, credentials, and charismatic gifts came, they fell under their spell. In this respect they were like the Galatians of whom Paul asked, "Who has bewitched you?" (Gal. 3:1).

As a matter of fact, Paul speaks somewhat the same in Galatians as he does in 2 Corinthians. He accuses the

Galatians, who have fallen under the hypnotic influence of certain troublers (Gal. 1:7; 3:1; 5:10, 12), of quickly transferring their allegiance from the One who called them in the grace of Christ to another gospel (1:6). He insists that the confusion stems from those who want to pervert the gospel of Christ (1:7), and he pronounces them accursed (1:8, 9). (Paul is thinking of Judaizers, Jewish Christians with a legalistic bent.)

The issue in Galatians is whether one is justified by works of law, chiefly circumcision, or by faith in the Cross of Christ. If this is also the issue in 2 Corinthians, Paul does not say so. Except for speaking about Moses and the letter of the law in 2 Corinthians 3, there is no mention of the law or of circumcision, which we would expect if the issue were the same.

As for the Cross, which Paul emphasizes so strongly in Galatians (1:4; 2:20, 21; 3:1; 5:20; 6:12, 14), it is highlighted in 2 Corinthians but not so much in terms of the centerpiece in an argument over legalism. In a context where Paul needed reconciliation with his converts, the death of Christ for all is mentioned as that event in which, through Christ becoming sin for us, God reconciles the world to Himself (2 Cor. 5:18-21). The Cross is also that event that is stamped upon the ministry of Paul (4:8-11). It seems clear that the Corinthians, and in particular, the protagonists of the different gospel, did not view the Cross as the emblem of suffering and shame to be imprinted upon their lives and which, by its reconciling power, made everyone equal. They had not allowed the Cross to alter their class consciousness and feeling of superiority to others.

For Paul the gospel of the Cross was the great leveler of all mankind, showing that humans were sinners unable to save themselves. Paul's Corinthian critics, however, saw themselves as anything but insufficient. The Cross, as an event of lowliness, had not seeped into their lives so as to create humility within them and a sense of human weakness within their ministry. The Cross just did not operate as a cross for them. They missed its significance, for they were too interested in the charismatic powers of the Spirit. Since they found it difficult to connect the Spirit with the Cross, as did Paul, they were really presenting a different Spirit than he did (11:4).

Though we wish we had more details about the views of Paul's opponents, we can make this generalization from what we do know. Sometimes even when people say they believe in Jesus and the gospel and have received the Spirit, they may be far from the New Testament meaning of those terms. They may even be using them in a way that undermines the meaning given by God's apostle. To avoid incorrect and deceptive views we need to expend time and energy studying Scripture in depth.

Regardless of whether Paul's opponents in Galatians and 2 Corinthians had the same theology, in Paul's estimation they did have some points very much in common. They had the same type of self-emphasis and competing spirit and played to Paul's converts in much the same way and to the same ends. The disturbers of the peace in Galatia quite likely are those implied in Paul's statements: "Let us not become conceited, competing against one another, envying one another" (Gal. 5:26) and "If, however, you bite and devour one another, take care that you are not devoured by one another" (5:15). The context of these statements shows them to be more than general instruction. They presuppose the activity of Paul's opponents who were pushing circumcision (5:1-6), preventing the Galatians from obeying the truth (5:7), and confusing them (5:10). Apart from the issue of circumcision, the stress on self-appraisal and attempts at seduction are quite similar in Galatians and Corinthians.

As to the goals Paul's opponents had in mind, these are also alike. The opponents in Galatia wanted the Galatians to follow their stipulations "so that they may boast in your flesh" (6:13). They wanted to make Paul's adherents theirs. Galatians 4:17 puts it this way: "Their devotion to you has no praiseworthy motive; they simply want to cut you off from me, so that you may centre your attention on them" (*New Jerusalem Bible*).

Paul accuses them of worldly standards that are contrary to the Cross (Gal. 6:14, 15). The Corinthian adversaries also wanted to take over Paul's converts; boasting was their hallmark, and they operated according to the world (2 Cor. 11:18). Paul says the Corinthians submitted readily to the suggestions of his rivals (11:4) and also states: "For you put up with it when someone makes slaves of you, or preys upon you, or takes advantage of you, or puts on airs, or gives you a slap in the face" (11:20). He sarcastically adds: "Pardon me for the shame of being too 'weak' to do the same!" (11:21, paraphrase mine).

Paul wonders why the Corinthians move away from him and submit so easily to his adversaries, since he is not in any way inferior to them (11:4, 5), a theme he will enlarge on in verses 21-33. He may not have the training they do in the higher forms of oratory, but this does not make him inferior, since he is very well trained in knowledge, as had to be evident to the Corinthians in every way (11:6). Obviously, there are two sets of standards here. The rival apostles reveled in oratorical ability that Paul did not have and on that point thought themselves superior to him. For Paul, the knowledge of the crucified Christ was much more important, and his manner of speaking comported with that knowledge: "When I came to you, brothers and sisters, I did not come proclaiming the mystery of God to you in lofty words or wisdom. For I decided to know nothing among you except Jesus Christ, and him crucified. And I came to you in weakness and in fear and in much trembling" (1 Cor. 2:1-3).

Proclaiming the gospel free of charge (2 Cor. 11:7-12)

The Corinthians believed in the patronage system operative in their culture. The wealthy were the patrons who paid clients for their loyal service. Paul was not about to be straitjacketed in that way and so refused patronage money. He wanted the independence to speak the gospel message under the direction of no one but Christ and was bent on representing the free nature of grace by giving the message of grace free of charge (1 Cor. 9:18). This was a real sore point with the Corinthians.

Their idea was that you could expect good service if a client was paid, but one who would refuse to receive payment would in effect be saying, "I don't have to give you my best." This is precisely what they thought of Paul. Instead of being thankful for his free service—after all, how often in life is something free?—they were angry. All itinerant philosophers got paid. Some of them even begged. Paul's rivals had accepted, even demanded, financial aid (implied in 2 Cor. 11:20), so what was wrong with Paul? They concluded that he must have an inferior product, was robbing them of the power and prestige that were attached to giving in Roman society, and was rejecting their friendship. At that time friendship was seen as the result of receiving, not as the cause. What this added up to was that Paul did not love them.

Not only did Paul not receive remuneration; he worked with his hands, making tents (Acts 18:3; 1 Cor. 4:12). Such manual labor was poorly regarded by the higher-ups in ancient society. Paul was clearly an embarrassment to some. He alludes to this when he asks in 2 Cor. 11:7, "Did I commit a sin by humbling myself?" meaning by working as a craftsman. He says he did this to exalt the Corinthians, that is, to place no burden on them (11:9). The fact that he asks if it was a sin for him not to receive their money, but to work with his hands to support himself, shows just how seriously they took his actions. Today, many of us would gladly receive money from others so as to avoid sin!

But here comes another point that stuck in their craw. Paul refused to receive their money, but he received money from others—from their longstanding rivals in Philippi, who were in a state of poverty (8:2). Writing to the Philippians he says: "When I was in Thessalonica, you sent me help for my needs more than once" (Phil. 4:16). Furthermore, they alone helped him when he left Macedonia (4:15). In fact, when he was ministering in the city of Corinth itself, his needs that went beyond his earnings were met by funds from Macedonia (2 Cor. 11:9).

How well I remember the help of the saints in my home

church when I was forced to leave home because I had become an Adventist. I went to college and worked but never could work enough to pay my bill. Money mysteriously poured in from my church to keep me going. Moreover, I was completely unprepared in terms of clothes and other necessities to function as a college student, but because of the generosity of my church family, my send-off included a large box of everything I needed. As I reflect on this, I feel somewhat like Paul, who received voluntary love gifts from his friends so he could continue to labor for Christ.

In any case, Paul received support from others but refused help from the Corinthians. He declares that he robbed others to serve the Corinthians. Of course, he didn't literally rob other churches, but he was willing to receive voluntary support from them so he would not burden the Corinthians (2 Cor. 11:8). Apparently it was his missionary policy never to receive aid from those he was directly working for but to be willing to receive some aid, if he needed it, after he went to a new area of evangelism.

What Paul hadn't realized, apparently, was just how negatively the Corinthians would react to his radical repudiation of a cherished social convention. He was firm in his resolve, however, and even after learning of their concern, his refusal stood.

Why? Paul gives two reasons. First, so his "boast" of making the gospel free of charge would not be silenced throughout the province of Achaia, of which Corinth was a part (11:10). He asks if this proves he does not love them. His answer is "God knows I do!" (11:11). Second, he did not wish to give his critics, who eagerly accepted such aid, an opportunity to claim that he and they were on a par, since he accepted such aid too. If his antagonists wanted to boast of such support, he would be glad to boast that he didn't accept it!

Unmasking the enemy (2 Cor. 11:13-15)
There comes a time when error needs to be unmasked, sin called by its right name, and false pretensions of those

who make much of themselves exposed. It is the spirit of the Jesus who expelled the money-changers rather than the meek and gentle Jesus that speaks here. Paul minces no words.

He had already sarcastically called his antagonists "super-apostles" (2 Cor. 11:5), mimicking how they thought of themselves. Now he contends that they are really false apostles, deceitful workers, disguising themselves as apostles of Christ (11:13). He declares that this should not surprise anyone, for Satan himself is a master of disguise, masquerading as an angel of light (11:14).

This seems as bad as things can get, but now Paul presents the coup de grace. These new missionaries are not merely like Satan; they are *his* ministers pretending to be ministers of righteousness! What's more, Paul now announces the doom of these false apostles. With true apostolic authority he passes sentence upon them: "Their end will match their deeds" (11:15). Paul's critics were right—his letters were bold!

Up fool's hill

Paul is about to give a speech in which he, carrying out his desire to speak foolishly (3:1), repeatedly describes himself as a fool (11:16, 17, 21; 12:11. In 11:23 "fool" is replaced by "madman," a fool gone mad). Strangely, he begins his fool's speech with the assertion, "Let no one think that I am a fool" (11:16). The reason he can say this is that he will be telling the truth (12:6) when playing the fool's role by boasting, and boasting even in suffering. In a really sarcastic remark, he says he is buoyed up to play the role of fool, "for you gladly put up with fools, being wise yourselves!" (11:19). If, in their wisdom, they can put up with the fools who are leading them astray, taking their money, and slapping them around (11:20), they ought to be able to put up with his foolish boasting!

Paul intends to prove that, rather than being inferior, as they claimed, he is actually superior to the self-styled apostles. Four areas of proof are offered. The first has to do with Judaic background. The super-apostles claimed that they were Hebrews, that is, were of the right blood, came from the motherland, and could speak the mother tongue. They also laid claim to being Israelites and descendants of Abraham, meaning they were bona fide members of the chosen people of God through whom blessing would come to the whole world.

On all counts Paul could say the same. His retort was, "So am I." It might seem difficult to see how he was a true Hebrew since he was born in Tarsus, but as he says in Acts 22:3, though born in Tarsus, he was brought up in Jerusalem. As to the Hebrew language, on one occasion in Jerusalem he made a defense of himself in Hebrew, and "when they heard him addressing them in Hebrew, they became even more quiet" (Acts 22:2). Indeed, as he says in Philippians 3:5, he was "a Hebrew born of Hebrews." He was also a member of God's chosen people. He explicitly calls himself an Israelite and, as for being a child of Abraham, he had the mark, for the sign of Abrahamic descendants was circumcision, and he was circumcised the eighth day (Phil. 3:5). As to lineage he does not come one whit behind the puffed up missionaries.

The second area of proof had to do with being a minister of Christ. In comparison with his challengers, he was a better one, for he put his life on the line for Christ. His credentials were the labors and toils, dangers and deprivations, sufferings and near-death experiences he endured. Indeed, as he says elsewhere, he bears in his body the wounds of Jesus (Gal. 6:17).

Listen to his hardship list, which exceeds what we have known about him from the account of his life in Acts.

> I've worked much harder, been jailed more often, beaten up more times than I can count, and at death's door time after time. I've been flogged five times with the Jews' thirty-nine lashes, beaten by Roman rods three times, pummeled with rocks once. I've been shipwrecked three times, and immersed in the open

sea for a night and a day. In hard traveling year in and year out, I've had to ford rivers, fend off robbers, struggle with friends, struggle with foes. I've been at risk in the city, at risk in the country, endangered by desert sun and sea storm, and betrayed by those I thought were my brothers. I've known drudgery and hard labor, many a long and lonely night without sleep, many a missed meal, blasted by the cold, naked to the weather (2 Cor. 11:23-27, *The Message*).

Then he says, besides everything else he has gone through, he is under pressure every day because of his anxiety for his churches (11:28). This was almost an intolerable burden. Anyone would feel weak before it. That is why he asks "Who is weak, and I am not weak?" The Corinthians didn't like the thought of weakness; it was power that allured them, but Paul believes weakness is an essential component of his ministry. That is why he catalogued his sufferings for them. Among the weak in the world he is the weakest of all! He has not only his personal difficulties to deal with but the weaknesses in his churches weigh him down as well.

He then rhetorically asks "Who is made to stumble, and I am not indignant?" While he admits to being weak in terms of the degree of his sufferings and pressure in ministry, he does this for his converts. Now, if his converts stumble because of the witness of the false apostles, what else could he feel but indignation? He feels a holy wrath when, in the language of Matthew 18, one of these little ones is caused to stumble.

Paul is not through descending to the bottom of the pit of weakness. He whose letters were strong (2 Cor. 10:10), whose face to face encounters could be strong as well (10:11), and who used military imagery to suggest the victories he could win (10:3-6), now deepens the sense of his weakness by referring to an event of humiliation. He announces his intention to do this in verse 30: "If I must boast, I will boast of the things that show my weakness."

There follows the story of an incident in Damascus when

he had to be secretly dropped in a basket out of a window in the wall so as to escape from the hands of King Aretas, who had put the city under guard in order to capture him. Quite a contrast to Roman soldiers who received awards for being first over the wall to meet the enemy. Paul was first over the wall to flee the captor! What humiliation for an apostle of Jesus Christ!

This brief story, which completes the catalogue of his sufferings, is the prelude to the story of his being taken up into heaven in 2 Corinthians 12:1-4. The apostle of humiliation also knows exaltation, for he is in the service of the One who left the throne of heaven to be nailed to an earthly cross but was exalted to heaven as a result of following His Father's will (Phil. 2:6-11).

The desire for personal power
is wrongheaded, completely at odds
with the gospel of the crucified Christ.

Chapter 12

2 Corinthians 12

POWER AND WEAKNESS

Visions and revelations (2 Cor. 12:1-6)

It is remarkable how many shifts and tensions there were in Paul's experiences. In the present passage we see him transported to high heaven yet discovering he had to feel a thorn on earth. His unexpected heavenly elevation was matched by the necessity of an earthy vexation. Though he could reveal no words from heaven, on earth he clearly heard heavenly words saying, "My grace is sufficient for you" (12:9).

Second Corinthians 11 ended with a man being lowered down a wall to escape an enemy. Chapter 12 begins with a man being exalted to heaven to meet his Lord. As Paul introduces this man, who did not really want to boast, he says, "It is necessary to boast" (12:1). If boasting is necessary, we would expect Paul to give us the rationale for it, but we are immediately disappointed. Having announced the necessity of boasting, he now declares its uselessness! Does Paul have a kind of schizophrenia, or is there something more to this picture? Why would useless boasting be used?

The answer is not far off. His opponents boasted (11:18, 21) and, as the present context implies, they boasted of divine revelation and ecstatic experiences. Throughout 2 Corinthians 11 Paul has been demonstrating that he is not inferior to these "super-apostles." So, in order to impress his wavering congregation, he resorts to what in principle is useless but in practice may sometimes be needed. Paul is willing therefore to "go on to visions and revelations of the Lord" (12:1).

Visionary experiences were not new to Paul. The book of Acts records several. After being blinded by the revelation of Christ, he had a vision that Ananias would touch his eyes, and he would see again (Acts 9:12). Interestingly enough, Ananias had a vision telling him to help Paul, for he was God's chosen vessel to reveal His name. He also saw that God would reveal to Paul how much he must suffer for the sake of His name (9:10-16).

In the very city of Corinth, Paul had a vision telling him to take courage because God had many people there (Acts 18:9, 10). A vision directed him to mission work in Macedonia (16:9, 10), and visions giving impetus to mission were connected with his first trip to Jerusalem after his conversion (22:17-21) and his last trip there (23:11). He even had a vision encouraging him to be unafraid when he appeared before Caesar as a prisoner (27:23, 24).

These visions are all connected with mission, but the vision recounted in 2 Corinthians 12 is unique in that, unlike the visions in Acts, which contain specific content, we learn little more about this vision than that it happened.

In speaking about this transcendent experience, Paul says "I know a person" and does not identify that person as himself. Why not? Probably because he really did not want to talk about himself, but feeling forced to it because of his rivals' claims, he wanted to mute its glory by speaking humbly in the third person.

He speaks of this person as being "in Christ." This is perhaps the most important phrase in Paul's writings. It occurs a total of one hundred sixty-four times, with 1 Corinthians containing twenty-three occurrences and 2 Corinthians thirteen. At rock bottom this phrase refers to the deepest personal union and communion with the crucified and risen Christ through the Spirit by which all the blessings of salvation are made accessible to the believer. It also refers to inclusion in the body of Christ where these blessings are celebrated.

A look at the many appearances of the "in Christ" phrases shows that every single aspect of Christian existence is contained in it, good and bad. Even Paul's bonds are "in Christ" (Phil. 1:13)! Paul, who summarized Christian existence in "For me to live is Christ" (Phil. 1:21, KJV) saw *nothing* that happens to the believer as outside of Christ. We are in Him, and He is in us, and that connection is not broken even in death, for Paul speaks of the "dead in Christ" (1 Thess. 4:16). In short, those "in Christ" live, move, and have their being in Him (compare Acts 17:28). They are believers, Christians, members of the body of Christ.

Concerning himself as a person who is "in Christ," Paul says that he had an experience fourteen years ago. This must have been a very notable experience, since he tells us nothing about the other revelations he had. Fourteen does not indicate a precise date but points to a definite happening that occurred well before Paul came to Corinth in the fifties A. D. Fourteen years earlier brings us back to the early forties, a period in Paul's life about which we know very little, except that he was witnessing to Jesus (Gal. 1:21, 22). In this period of obscurity Paul received the clarity of divine revelation.

Paul is not sure how it happened, whether physically or in some spiritual, ecstatic state ("whether in the body or out of the body"—2 Cor. 12:2, 3), but he was caught up to the third heaven, which is the region of Paradise (12:2-4). This is where Jesus said he would meet the thief on the cross (Luke 23:43). It is also the place where the tree of life is found (Rev. 2:7). While in this heavenly world he heard things that no mortal was allowed to repeat (2 Cor. 12:4). Ellen White comments:

> Paul had a view of heaven, and in discoursing on the glories there, the very best thing he could do was to not try to describe them. He tells us that eye had not seen nor ear heard, neither hath it entered into the heart of man the things which God hath prepared for those that love Him. So you may put your imagination to the

stretch, you may try to the very best of your abilities to take in and consider the eternal weight of glory, and yet your finite senses, faint and weary with the effort, cannot grasp it, for there is an infinity beyond. It takes all of eternity to unfold the glories and bring out the precious treasures of the Word of God (*SDA Bible Commentary*, 6:1107).

When Paul describes what happened, he does not emphasize what is seen but what is heard, though he is not at liberty to repeat it to anyone. He is the special and private repository of heaven's secrets. Here is a man in touch with God. There is an aura of mystery about it, calling the Corinthians to place their faith in one who walked heaven's streets, heard its sounds, and communed with the Lord Himself.

Paul continues by saying that he will boast of this person who went to heaven, but then, as if distancing himself from him, says that on his own behalf he will not boast except in weakness. This was a rebuke to his opponents, who were interested only in power. The next words are also directed against them. Paul says he will refrain from boasting "so that no one will think better of me than what is seen in me or heard from me" (12:6). Though Paul did not want his converts to underestimate him, he also did not want them to overestimate him, as they were doing with the super-apostles. What the Corinthians needed to know was not really the content of his heavenly revelation but the gospel message they heard him give and saw him demonstrate before their eyes.

Paul is very clear that out-of-the-ordinary charismatic experiences cannot be the basis for our Christianity or witness. The proclamation of the crucified Christ by those who are dead to the world and self, and the upbuilding of others in love—these are the marks of the true servant of Jesus. As 1 Corinthians 13 teaches, even if one could speak with the tongues not only of humans but of angels, but had no love for others, it would count for nothing. The same is true for the gift of prophecy and miracle-working faith. Without love, these gifts have no true content.

Strength in weakness (2 Cor. 12:7-10)

The necessity of evaluating him in terms of his everyday message and mission is true, he says, "even considering the exceptional character of the revelations" he had experienced (12:6, 7). The Greek word behind "exceptional" here (*hyperbole*)—a word having to do with excess—refers either to the high quality of his revelations (as in the NRSV translation above) or to the manifold quantity of the revelations, as in the KJV and RSV. Both ideas are undoubtedly involved.

Paul had many incredible revelations, like the one he recounts in 12:2-4, and to keep him from being too exalted or conceited by them—a strike at the haughty spirit of the super-apostles—he was given a thorn in the flesh, a messenger of Satan, to torment him. This is an amazing statement. God makes use of Satan's work to keep Paul humble! As in the Old Testament story of the treachery of Joseph's brothers, what was intended for evil was used by God for good (Gen. 50:20). That was the effect of the thorn (which could be translated "stake," a sharply pointed stick or instrument) as well.

To have a thorn in the flesh is obviously to have a very painful experience, which could be physical, emotional, or both. Some think it could even be the pain suffered from bad relationships like Paul had with his Corinthian critics. In this case, "thorn in the flesh" might mean something like "pain in the neck."

Many specific proposals have been offered to explain what Paul meant. These include epilepsy, malaria, eye trouble, migraine headaches, depression, and the like. We have some clues about the trouble from Galatians. Paul says that it was because of a physical infirmity that he first preached the gospel to them, and they welcomed him as they would an angel, or even Christ Jesus. So close and sympathetic were they to him that they would even have torn out their eyes and given them to him if that would have helped (Gal.

4:13, 15). Then at the letter's end, written by Paul rather than the scribe he had been employing, he points to his large printing as he writes in his own hand (6:11). Perhaps he wrote in large letters because he wanted to emphasize what he was saying, but it may have been because his eyesight was poor. Ellen White says:

> Paul had a bodily affliction; his eyesight was bad. He thought that by earnest prayer the difficulty might be removed. But the Lord had His own purpose, and He said to Paul, "Speak to Me no more of this matter. My grace is sufficient. It will enable you to bear the infirmity" (SDA *Bible Commentary*, 6:1107).

It may well be that accompanying Paul's bad eyesight—which could have contributed to the impression that his bodily presence was weak (2 Cor. 10:10)—were terribly painful, periodic headaches. This would fit with the idea of something sharp jabbing him. This could have been a residual effect from the blinding experience on the Damascus road when he met the risen Christ.

As Jesus three times asked His Father to let the cup of suffering pass from Him (Mark 14:32-42), so Paul prayed three times that the Lord would remove this affliction (2 Cor. 12:8). The Lord answered negatively, saying: "My grace is sufficient for you, for power is made perfect in weakness" (12:9).

Our prayers are not always answered as we wish. Moses prayed to go into the Promised Land but died alone on a mountain looking into the land. The author of Psalm 88 prayed to be delivered from a death-dealing illness, but the psalm ends with no indication of healing or any direct answer at all. Jesus prayed that the cup might pass, but He had to drink it. Paul prayed for the pain to go away, but it did not. God's thoughts and purposes are higher than ours. He does not always give us what we ask for, but we can always count on Him to give us what we really need.

While discussing the story of the leper in Luke 5:12-28,

Ellen White makes some very relevant comments on prayer. She says that "in some instances of healing, Jesus did not at once grant the blessing sought. . . . When we pray for earthly blessings, the answer to our prayer may be delayed, or God may give us something other than we ask" (*The Desire of Ages*, 266). This was the case in all the prayer requests mentioned above.

However, Ellen White continues by stating that there is one prayer that we can be certain will always receive an immediate Yes. That is the prayer for deliverance from sin. "It is His will to cleanse us from sin, to make us His children, and to enable us to live a holy life" (ibid.). This is a comprehensive answer involving forgiveness, adoption, and sanctification. It is wonderful to know that we need not wait for these gifts. They are ours now! It is the knowledge of this fact that can sustain us in our suffering.

That is why in the second half of Romans 8, where Paul is addressing the problem of suffering people, he speaks again about the death of Jesus for us, His justification of us, and intercession for us in heaven above (8:32-34). When everything seems arrayed against us, we can make it if we know that God is for us, and none of life's separating factors can divide us from His love (8:35-39).

In this particular context the word *grace* in God's answer to Paul—"My grace is sufficient for you"—must be a reference to God's power, for the second half of the sentence says "for power is made perfect in weakness." Grace can be the unmerited favor of God's forgiveness, but it can also mean the unmerited favor of His empowerment. (For Paul, even the commission to be an apostle was a manifestation of grace—Rom. 1:5.)

When God announces that His grace or power are sufficient for us, it is not a declaration of immunity to trouble and pain. Rather, we are to understand that His power is sufficient to get us through adversity. Thus the weakness we feel when we suffer is neither replaced nor quelled by God's power; we still continue to feel weak. But God's power is perfected—comes to its fullest expression—in our continuing weakness. Paradoxically, our weakness is a conveyance for God's power. The treasure of the gospel will always be in earthen vessels, so that it may continually be seen that the transcendent power belongs to Him and not to us (2 Cor. 4:7). Weakness and suffering will never leave us, but neither will God's gracious power. It is that which, in the midst of trial and deepest pain, "transfigures you and me."

That is why Paul says that he will "all the more gladly" boast of his weaknesses, for it is then that the power of Christ rests upon him (12:9). This is a reference to the resurrection power that God manifested in Christ when He raised Him from the dead and that is now manifested through the risen Christ for our sakes. The power of Christ dwelling in the believer is the reality that accompanies him in his weakness each and every day.

Because Christ and His power dwell in the suffering Christian, Paul is able to declare: "Therefore, I am content with weaknesses, insults, hardships, persecutions, and calamities for the sake of Christ; for whenever I am weak, then I am strong" (12:10). What this is really saying—and Paul's rivals needed to take note—is that the desire for personal power is wrongheaded, completely at odds with the gospel of the crucified Christ. Our weakness, with the suffering it entails and the necessary dependence upon God it requires, is the form that the Cross takes now. It is the prerequisite for the working of resurrection power. God is the One who, in the midst of death, raises the dead (1:9).

Divine strength in human weakness is the theme of 2 Corinthians, and "To God be the glory" is the watchword of the Christian. God is the power behind human existence, gospel witness, and congregational fitness. When, despite human frailty, this power is extolled through the lips of those God has redeemed, the Cross becomes the power of God for salvation to everyone who believes.

God was everything to Paul. In view of his sinfulness and weakness he was like a dead man hanging on a cross, but God was his life.

Chapter 13

2 Corinthians 12:11–13:13

CONCERNS AND WARNINGS

It has been said that the best defense is a good offense. Paul has been the defendant on trial in almost all of 2 Corinthians. Now in the last part of the book, the heat will be on the Corinthians. They have things to answer for. So, while 12:1-10 could have been an excellent ending for the book, because it powerfully emphasizes Paul's theme of strength in weakness, he continues to write, hoping that by the close of the letter they will have stopped criticizing him and started focusing on reversing their lives and making their entire way of thinking captive to Christ.

The signs of an apostle (2 Cor. 12:11, 12)
From 11:21–12:10 Paul has been making what he calls "a fool's speech." He is now done and admits that in giving such a speech he is a fool. But, he tells his converts, "You forced me to it!" The Corinthian congregation caused trouble rather than solving it. They should have been commending him rather than forcing him to commend himself (12:11).

They would have had plenty of reason to commend him, too, for despite the allegations of his opponents, the signs of a true apostle were performed among them. Paul does not say "I performed them" but uses the passive voice, thus taking the emphasis off himself and placing it on God. Throughout his ministry, divinely wrought signs, wonders, and mighty works were in evidence (compare Gal. 3:5 and Rom.

132

15:18, 19). The presence of the miraculous was seen and felt. Apparently the super-apostles had appealed to such things to validate their ministry, otherwise Paul would not have had to argue that he was not inferior to those claiming feats of power.

We know, however, that Paul did not put much stock in things like this. Rather, he underlined his weakness that cast God's power into bold relief. That's why he tosses into his argument two interesting little phrases. The first is in 2 Corinthians 12:11. While contending that he is not in the least inferior to his critics, he says "though I am nothing." Whose estimate was this? It summarizes precisely what his rivals thought of him, but he takes ownership of it. When they focused upon themselves, they thought they were great. When Paul looked at himself, he said "I am nothing."

As far as Paul was concerned, his persecution of the Christians, which was actually persecution of Jesus and blasphemy against God (Acts 9:4; in 1 Tim. 1:13), was evidence that he was the foremost of sinners (1 Tim. 1:15). In light of this, when he said it was God's grace alone that made him what he was (1 Cor. 15:10), he really meant it. Of himself he was nothing.

Perhaps that is why he compares his conversion to Creation, when God chased the darkness away by making light shine (2 Cor. 4:6) and why he thinks of justification—proclaimed and experienced by himself—as giving life to the dead and calling into existence the things that do not exist (Rom. 4:17). At one time he was only darkness, nothingness. However, God was everything to him. In view of his sinfulness and weakness, he was like a dead man hanging on a cross, but God was his life.

The second small phrase is found in 2 Corinthians 13:12. Just before recounting the signs of apostleship that accompanied his ministry, he says that these were performed among them "with utmost patience." Here is a pointer to Paul's endurance of trial and suffering, much of which came from the Corinthians! No matter what he went through and how much patience he had to exercise, the signs of God's

power were still there. These miraculous events were signs
of the new age that was breaking into a world filled with the
kind of suffering Paul went through (see 11:23-29 and 12:10)
and for which patient endurance was very much needed.

The burden of not burdening (2 Cor. 12:13-18)

Paul has been very concerned to demonstrate that there
was nothing lacking in his ministry for the Corinthians. But
according to them, there certainly was something lacking—
he did not allow them to give him money. He thereby defied
the social conventions of the time and deprived those who
wanted to be his patrons from the plaudits of the Christian
public.

So once again, as in 11:7-11, Paul speaks about the fact
that he never placed a financial burden upon his converts.
To have to speak about this again must have greatly dis-
tressed him. It also highlights the Corinthians' feeling of
injury about this, especially since he took aid from others.
So Paul asks them: "How have you been worse off than the
other churches, except that I myself [unlike the super-
apostles] did not burden you?" Then almost sarcastically he
declares, "Forgive me this wrong!" (12:13). There was a chill
in the air at this point. They could not understand him, and
he could not comprehend them. Pastor and parishioners were
like ships passing in the night.

At this late stage in the letter Paul remains adamant
yet affectionate. He tells them that he is about to come to
them a third time and continues to refuse their funds, for
"I do not want what is yours but you; for children ought
not to lay up for their parents, but parents for their children" (12:14). Paul reverses the Corinthians' expectations
for social order here. If he had accepted their patronage,
he would have been dependent upon them, but by speaking of himself as their father—rightly so—he makes them
dependent upon him.

"Not yours, but you"—what a wonderful policy for relationships! In the normal cultural desire for enrichment and
gain from others, it is unusual to hear someone say "All I

want from you is you." This is the Christian antidote to the pervasive perception in society that others want something from us but are not really interested in us for ourselves. In his inaugural speech John Kennedy stated: "Ask not what your country can do for you; ask what you can do for your country." That was Paul's perspective, and he was prepared to spend and be totally spent for his people (12:15).

However, the more he said things like this, the worse the situation became. Presuppositions and prejudice, culture and conditioning determine how people hear things. The Corinthians were still enmeshed in the culture of patron/client relationships and refused to cut that tie and be crucified to their world. Thus things were bad and getting worse on the point of Paul's rejection of pay. He plaintively asks: "If I have loved you more, am I to be loved less?" Paul has turned the tables here. They claimed that his refusal of help was evidence that he did not love them. He counters with "If I have shown my love by not burdening you, why do you withdraw your love from me?" (my paraphrase).

Just how bad things could become is indicated by a deeper charge against Paul. Some came up with a theory about a swindle on Paul's part. He rejected their support to cover up the fact that he was stealing from the offering he supposedly was taking to the poor in Jerusalem. They likely thought "Paul is enriching himself at our expense, all the while refusing our pay for his expenses." What a duplicitous dealer of darkness!

Paul points out that though he did not burden them, they say he is crafty and took them in by deceit. He was being charged with reaping personal benefit from the Jerusalem collection. He passionately asks whether he took advantage or defrauded them through those he sent to secure their commitment to give the offering and later to collect it. He had sent Titus and, most likely, the unnamed, earnest brother of 8:22. Had these two committed any fraud? The answer being negative, he asks whether he in any way had departed from the same principle of honesty (12:17, 18)? If you can't fault the disciples, why fault the master?

Defense, No! Building up, Yes! (2 Cor. 12:19-21)

To eradicate any thought in their minds, as they have read his letter, that he was on trial before them, Paul hastens to say that all he has written has been much more that just one long defense of himself. On a much deeper level, he has been standing before God, not them, and speaking the truth in Christ. This has been for one ultimate reason—to fulfill his apostolic commission to build up his congregation. Everything has been directed to that end (12:19). He has been intent on strengthening them because he fears that when he comes, he will not find them to be the kind of persons they ought to be. This has a reverse side, of course, for they might not find him to be as they wish (12:20).

First, he deals with his fear about them. He is deeply troubled, indicated by his use of "I fear" three times in two verses (20, 21). He fears that he will discover some of the problems he dealt with in previous letters and visits still going on. Among these are "quarreling, jealousy, anger, selfishness, slander, gossip, conceit, and disorder" (12:20). As if that weren't enough, he is afraid he will be humbled (humiliated) and have to mourn "over many who previously sinned and have not repented of the impurity, sexual immorality, and licentiousness they have practiced" (12:12).

Paul does not say he *will* find these things but that he *may* find them. The future is not already signed, sealed, and delivered. If any of these things are true of some of his converts—in verse 21 he fears that their numbers may reach "many"—they still have time before he comes to reverse their course and repent.

No lenience for impenitents (2 Cor. 13:1-4)

Now Paul deals with the other side of the coin—that if his converts don't measure up, he will not be what they wish. The same flame that warms may also burn. Paul wants to warm his converts with his love and acceptance, but apostleship deals not only with warming but also with warning and, if need be, discipline and punishment.

Paul, who so frequently characterized himself as a person of weakness, now utilizes shock therapy! As if in a pretrial hearing over the Corinthians' behavior, he cites the Old Testament law that "any charge must be sustained by the testimony of two witnesses" (Deut. 19:15). He believes he has the two witnesses required for his case. These witnesses tie in with his statement in 2 Corinthians 13:2 that he warned them before and is now warning them again. His first witness is the evidence he found on his painful visit that caused him to warn the Corinthians about their conduct. His second witness was the evidence that was leading him to warn them now in 2 Corinthians. This evidence was such that a third visit would not allow him to be lenient with them as he was before (2:1, 2). It was to spare them from severe judgment that he had not yet returned to Corinth. Although he doesn't want to do so (10:2; 13:10), he is now prepared to be stern (since his second visit showed that being nice didn't work) and to fulfill what he said about being "ready to punish every disobedience" (10:6).

The Corinthians had insisted on proof that Christ spoke in him. Paul will give them proof but of an altogether different kind than they demanded. Instead of ecstatic or miraculous manifestations, he will give them strong discipline! Christ, through His apostle, would be powerful (13:3). The time for gentle dealings with them was past. As Christ had been crucified in weakness, but now lives by the power of God, the same would be portrayed in Paul. He still experiences weakness in his walk "in Christ," but when he returns to Corinth he will live with Christ by the power of God (13:4). This refers to his present connection with Christ that will enable him to be a powerful disciplinarian for all who need it (see 1 Cor. 5:3-5).

Meeting the test (2 Cor. 13:5-11)

His converts have been examining him. Now Paul in effect says "Enough of that. Take your critical eyes off me and focus them on yourselves and prove whether you are genuinely 'living in the faith.'" Paul's concern is not merely with correct beliefs but about the practical effect of correct beliefs—"living in the faith." Theology and morality must always go hand in hand. Believing in Jesus is not just mental assent; it is practical godliness.

Interestingly, though Paul questions if his converts are living in the faith, he goes on to state that, unless they have already failed the test of genuineness, they must surely be aware that Jesus Christ is in them! (13:5). Here Paul is not contradicting himself but reestablishing the foundation for all Christian living. He makes the assumption that the Corinthians have a relationship with Christ. This is the basis for asking them to live in a way that honors Him.

"Living in the faith" is living obediently, the test he speaks about in 2:9. While in one sense faith in Christ gives rise to obedience to Him, in another, faith itself is obedience to Christ. Romans 1:5 speaks of "the obedience of faith," meaning "the obedience which is faith." Faith is the deepest act of obedience we can make. It calls for a total surrender to the verdict (we are sinners), the gift (Christ will save us), and the claim of God (we are called to follow Him as Lord). When Paul admonishes them to examine themselves to see if they are living in the faith, the object is to find if there is total conformity to Christ; whether every thought is "captive to obey Christ" (2 Cor. 10:5) and their "obedience is complete" (10:6).

Paul does not want them to fail this examination of genuineness (13:5) and correspondingly hopes they will find that he has not failed to be genuine, though in view of their present state he may *seem* to have failed (13:7). So closely linked is the success of his converts with his success as an apostle that if they fail (13:5), so will he (13:6). Their obedience is the only proof that their faith and his apostleship are genuine. Consequently, he is responsible for them, and they are responsible for him.

Paul is in a praying mode in this passage. Much is at stake. He needs God's power to manifest itself once again in his weakness so his converts will do nothing wrong, meaning that they will not reject his apostolic claims and moral instructions. This is not so he may be approved but so they will do what is right for its own sake, irrespective of whether or not he has seemed to fail (13:7). Paul is more concerned about their passing the test than with his own vindication, though he knows the latter depends on the former. He is optimistic about the outcome, however, and in a jab at the false apostles says that truth will prevail. No one can ultimately do anything against it, but only for it (13:8). Indeed, "truth marches on."

In this spirit he asserts that he rejoices if, when he is weak, they are strong in faith. He prays that they will be strengthened in such a way that they will be completely restored and healed (13:9) by making their repentance complete. Then when he comes, he will not have to be tough on them as he seeks to build them up (13:10).

There is an obvious question here about their repentance. If chapters 10–13 are part of the same letter as chapters 1–9, and in 7.5-10 Paul rejoices in their repentance, why is he still asking them to repent in chapter 13? The answer may lie in this. In chapter 7 the repentance they have manifested contains three elements: (1) a new concern and longing for Paul; (2) willingness to exercise discipline on one who had insulted him; and (3) the welcome of his emissary Titus and obedience to his directives. This was extremely valuable, but more had to be done. Chapter 13 makes it clear that they needed not only to care for Paul but to submit to his authority in Christ and cleanse themselves of any moral evils still present (see 12:20, 21).

Final appeal and prayer (2 Cor. 13:11-13)

As Paul closes his letter, he makes a number of summary appeals. First, he asks them to rejoice. A good relationship between them is still possible. He looks to the future in confidence. Furthermore, less criticism of him and more rejoicing in what he brought them will do all of them a lot of good. Marriages sometimes break down because people concentrate only on the negative. To look at and rejoice over the positive brings healing.

Second, he enjoins them to "put things in order," a translation that derives from the Greek word (*katartizo*) which means "to mend" (as fishermen do their nets or a doctor brings fractured bones together again). The word is a verb form of the noun used for restoration at the end of verse 9. Paul wants nothing more than for his congregation to find perfect healing.

Third, Paul entreats them to listen to his appeal. At this point the opening words of a well-known hymn are appropriate:

Softly and tenderly, Jesus is calling,
Calling for you and for me;
At the heart's portal He's waiting and watching,
Watching for you and for me.
(*Seventh-day Adventist Hymnal*, 287)

Finally, Paul admonishes them to manifest what he has been seeking ever since the beginning of 1 Corinthians: "Agree with one another" and "live in peace." This call to peace will not be vain if people grasp that the God of love and peace will be with them (2 Cor. 13:11). To fully accept God's love not only leads to peace with Him but peace with each other. Whereas in our world peace is the precondition for love, in Paul's mind love is the presupposition for peace. However, this love is first of all God's love for us. Reception of His love makes possible the extension of His love and peace to others. When this happens, love will become a river of peace flowing to the entire world.

Final greetings and prayer (2 Cor. 13:11-14)

Paul sends final greetings and then closes his letter with prayer. As he prayed for his converts in verses 7 and 9, he now offers a benedictory prayer, in Trinitarian form, with love as its centerpiece. Let us hear this prayer as not only for them but also for us today. In our weakness we need the strength and blessing of our triune God. "The grace of the Lord Jesus Christ, the love of God, and the communion of the Holy Spirit be with all of you." Amen!